The Eternal Flames

The Inspiring Story of the Stanley Cup-Winning Season

PETER MAHER WITH JOHN IABONI

M&S

McClelland & Stewart Inc.
The Canadian Publishers
481 University Avenue
Toronto, Ontario
M5G 2E9

CANADIAN CATALOGUING IN PUBLICATION DATA
Maher, Peter
    The eternal Flames

ISBN 0-7710-4306-6

1. Calgary Flames (Hockey team). 2. Stanley Cup
(Hockey). I. Iaboni, John. II. Title.

GV848.C28M3 1989   796.96'26   C89-095400-3

DESIGN: Brant Cowie/ArtPlus Limited

PAGE MAKE-UP: Dale Bateman/ArtPlus Limited

CALGARY SUN PHOTOS BY: Carlos Amat, Dave Chidley, Jack Cusano,
                    Mike Drew, John Gibbson, Dave Olecko

Printed and bound in Canada.

Contents

Acknowledgements

This project has truly been a labour of love. In the process, the two of us were once again reunited to collaborate on yet another hockey venture, by far our most exciting since first meeting on the NHL beat in 1978.

The greatest season in the history of the Flames deserved to be recaptured and remembered. We are most appreciative McClelland & Stewart Inc. provided us the opportunity to retell the story of *The Eternal Flames*.

We thank all those who participated in assisting us throughout this project, either in the gathering of information or in the selection and processing of the outstanding collection of photographs.

The encouragement from relatives, friends, colleagues, and fans was most overwhelming and much appreciated. Special thanks to Lanny McDonald, a very dear friend who wrote the Foreword to *The Eternal Flames*. Straight from the heart, classy – a winner.

Finally, we wish to acknowledge the understanding, patience, support, and love from our immediate families – Nancy, Jeff, and Tricia Maher … Ada and Matthew Iaboni.

Thank you.

Peter Maher and John Iaboni

Foreword
by Lanny McDonald

t is with great pride that I write the Foreword to this book for several reasons.

As a team, the Calgary Flames were able to come together, not only as individuals with a great amount of talent but a team spirit that came alive over the course of a six-week span in the spring of 1989 in that hockey marathon known as the Stanley Cup playoffs. That essential combination of heart and talent took us to the ultimate prize in the world of hockey – the Stanley Cup. Together, we fought for a common goal and, through many challenges, arrived to collect our prized possession that memorable evening in Montreal.

My pride in writing this also comes from the fact that the two gentlemen who wrote this book are friends of mine.

After arriving in Toronto in the fall of 1973 for my first NHL training camp, I was sitting in the darkened Maple Leaf Gardens, trying to grasp the enormity of it all, when a young reporter approached me requesting an interview. It was to be my first. I asked him to wait; I needed a few moments to myself. Looking back now, it was a very bold request! And being the man he was, he waited.

John Iaboni may never know how I appreciated his indulgence at that time, as well as his much-needed support over my struggling start with the Maple Leafs. We don't see each other very often, but when our paths do cross, it's always fun to sit and chat with an old friend.

Peter Maher was just beginning his career as an NHL play-by-play announcer when I was beginning to feel a part of the Maple Leafs, so our friendship goes back many years. We've reached so many of our own career milestones together. I was able to help

Peter celebrate the announcing of his 500th and 1,000th games and, in turn, he called my 500th goal and 1,000th point. I think anyone who has listened to Peter will agree there was nothing quite as exciting as Peter yelling his famous "Ya, Baby!" over the airwaves in the Flames' initial triumph over the mighty Oilers in 1986.

In this game, it is a great treasure to have a friend who is able to listen sincerely and understand the inside world of hockey. Well, Peter, thanks – we've been through a lot together!

In a lifetime, we all have our own dreams and aspirations and we all have our mountains to climb. You must set a goal and work toward it. It takes hard work, a determination of attitude, but, most of all, that climb demands the willingness to sacrifice. When an opportunity, such as the Stanley Cup playoffs, presents itself, it gives you the motivation to make that climb together – to aim for the top with your teammates, and your friends. And it is that battle that bonds you as one to reach for that common goal.

The feelings shared over the course of a year are not always joyful: there is the disappointment of losing; the personal struggles a player must endure as part of a group, but really, completely alone. Experiences like these help to weld friendships and memories that last a lifetime.

Those who know, say there's nothing like winning your first Stanley Cup. I'm sure they're right! If ever there were a feeling of peace, it came with holding that Stanley Cup high above my head. For years, I had watched others hold the coveted silverware, but now, it was *our* turn ... life was ever so sweet!

They say one of God's greatest gifts is that of memories. So, Peter and John, thank you for writing this book – I know it will be terrific because this is one great memory!

Night of the Eternal Flames

hey are indeed *The Eternal Flames*.

The night was Thursday, May 25, 1989, and as the Calgary Flames meticulously extinguished the Montreal Canadiens at the fabled Montreal Forum, they finally gained the accolades and honours many doubted they could – or would – ever possess.

Joe Nieuwendyk, battered by a broken wrist, slashed during that decisive 4–2 triumph on the momentous night, and barely over the effects of a tongue seriously cut and stitched in the Clarence Campbell Conference final against Chicago, exemplified the guts, determination, and pride of all Flames on this mission of 1988-89. He played in pain, he played with inspiration, and he played intent on reaching that elusive goal that guarantees perpetuity for the Flames.

"Before the Montreal series, all the talk was about the Canadiens and all their history," Nieuwendyk said amid the post-game celebration in the Flames' dressing room. "Well, we made history here tonight!"

They had much to prove – to their fans, to the world, and to themselves. They had a mission, for their fans and for themselves. The Flames completed the National Hockey League's gruelling 80-game schedule with more points than any other team for the second consecutive season. But capturing that Presidents' Trophy was by no means their number-one goal. It represented that monumental first step, nothing more.

Their winning of the Clarence Campbell Bowl as champions of their conference became the second acquisition. That guaranteed them a spot in the Stanley Cup Final, nothing more.

How bent were they on chasing the ultimate prize and keeping the lid on along the way? Enough even to reject the free champagne offered by the Los Angeles Marriott Hotel after their sweep of the Los Angeles Kings. To a man, they claimed that the only time they wanted to taste the bubbly was after winning the Stanley Cup. They were a team obsessed with that final victory.

For the franchise, it represented the first Stanley Cup championship in a 17-year history that began in the Deep South (Atlanta) in 1972 and carried on to Calgary in 1980. For Cliff Fletcher, the president and general manager of the Flames and the man who built the club from the very beginning, it was the culmination of a task well done ... the best of times after some very worst of times. Never, though, did he or others involved with the team give up.

"I'm really happy ... 16 years of waiting for next year and finally next year arrived," Fletcher said. "It's a great feeling and we're going to savour this for a long time. I'm so proud of everyone in the organization. I'm so happy for all the fans back in Calgary because, believe me, this Cup's for them."

For Lanny McDonald, it was that final dream he'd chased through 16 NHL seasons. Fans across Canada followed his every step along the way as one of Canada's most recognizable – and well-liked – personalities capped off his career in a flurry that resulted in his 500th goal, 1,000th point, and a final career goal at the Forum (which was the site of his first NHL goal in 1973) on that Stanley Cup winning night. At long last, McDonald carried that beautiful trophy around the ice.

"It's the most peaceful feeling in the world," Lanny would tell me on the QR77 post-game show. "But it's the greatest. It was a lot of hard work but it all comes down to winning and I'm sure glad we won. The personal goals are very nice but they don't mean a thing unless you win the Stanley Cup. The personal things are bonuses along the way ... this tops it all off."

On the same post-game session, Fletcher paid tribute to Lanny in this manner: "Let's face it, Lanny gave our franchise credibility when we so desperately needed it back in the 1981-82 season with the Edmonton Oilers emerging as a great team. He provided us with leadership on the ice and off the ice. He is a great community figure so he's been the most important thing to ever happen to this franchise."

Lanny McDonald never placed himself ahead of the team. When the championship moment finally came on Forum ice he maintained that one-for-all posture. He asked his co-captains, Jim Peplinski and Tim Hunter, who were not in uniform for that final game, to come onto the ice and become part of the festivities.

The scene on that muggy night at the Forum was literally a far cry from 1986, when tears of disappointment followed the Flames' loss to the Canadiens. On national television and again on our post-game show in 1986, McDonald's emotional outburst conveyed the heartbreak of defeat. And yet while it was a down time in a brilliant career for both Lanny and his family, who waited for him late into that night at the Saddledome, the touch of class that has become his trademark remained.

I was amazed to see, as Lanny headed out that back door of the Saddledome still wiping away the tears, a group of some 25 youngsters clamouring for his autograph. All Lanny did was stop and sign every one of those autographs at a time when I'm sure all he wanted to do was get away from the building and be somewhere else so he could express his disappointment in losing.

But the tears shed in 1989 were those of joy because Lanny's prayers, and those of his close-knit family, were answered in what his wife Ardell termed "the best moment in hockey."

"I knew he could do it," Ardell said of Lanny's goal in the decisive game. "I think he probably said a million times tonight that he scored his first goal here and his last goal here. I'm glad I was here to see them both." Her comments ended when she and Lanny embraced.

Several times during the 1988-89 season, Lanny let it slip that retirement was on the horizon. He had gone from ace goal scorer to role player over the past three years but constantly concealed the hurt he may have had when not playing. He was a surprise starter in the deciding game against Montreal, only receiving the nod to play 20 minutes before the game. He had missed three games before that decision was made and he responded in typical McDonald fashion by giving everything he had.

"When I was put into the lineup, my first thought was I didn't just want to be in the lineup, I wanted to help make a difference," he said. "Regardless of whether you score or not, you can be a leader in a lot of ways. Whether it's through aggressiveness or just talking to the guys and being up. I wanted to be a factor, especially in the physical part of the game and, hopefully, tire some of their defencemen out. The goal was a bonus."

As the Flames gained momentum toward the Stanley Cup triumph, the snowball grew to the point more and more people would say, "Gee, it would be great for Lanny to finally win that Stanley Cup."

"Forget the 'let's win the ring for Lanny' stuff, the thing is we won it for everybody," McDonald said afterwards. "That really used to tick me off."

During the summer of 1989, after the Cup win, McDonald announced his retirement, news that had long been anticipated but nonetheless was difficult to accept. The McDonald story ended with the Flames atop the hockey world, having in the process become the first team to defeat the Canadiens in a Final series on Forum ice.

"It's funny, Nieuwy (Joe Nieuwendyk) kept on saying, 'Let's start our own tradition, to hell with Forum tradition.' It was great," McDonald said.

The Calgary Flames of 1988-89 represented an organization worthy of the NHL championship. The city of Calgary, which staged the most successful Olympic Winter Games in 1988, rarely has basked in pro title glory by the Stampeders of the Canadian Football League and never, until 1989, that of the NHL's Flames. In the 76 years of the Grey Cup championship, Calgarians have watched the Stampeders win but twice – 1948 and 1971 – in only five championship appearances. There is small consolation in the fact the Grey Cup's week-long festivities are attributed to the 1948 championship in Toronto, when Calgarians by trainloads introduced Hogtown to chuckwagons, pancake breakfasts, and horses in hotel lobbies. It was, by all accounts, quite a party and a new dimension to the Grey Cup festivities.

The province of Alberta is fortunate to have fashioned quite a great Canadian sporting tradition, thanks to the spirit it possesses and largely due to Calgary's rival neighbours to the north, Edmonton. While the Stampeders have produced few Grey Cup titles, the Edmonton Eskimos have garnered 10 Grey Cup wins (including an unprecedented five consecutive from 1978 through 1982) in 18 Grey Cup games. The Oilers, who made their NHL debut in 1979 with the greatest player in the world at the helm in Wayne Gretzky, emerged as the second dominant force of the 1980s once they wrestled the Stanley Cup away from the New York Islanders' four-year dynasty. The Oilers were Stanley Cup finalists in 1983 and winners in 1984, 1985, 1987, and 1988.

The high of Calgary's ouster of the Oilers during the 1986 Stanley Cup derby became sidetracked when the Canadiens defeated the Flames in five games to win the Stanley Cup Final. It was believed then that the time had not yet arrived for the Flames to reign supreme. The Oilers had, after all, lost the Final in 1983 before gaining the coveted Cup in 1984 and 1985. What Calgarians anticipated was a demise in the Oilers and a rise in the Flames, but in 1987 the Oilers were back in Stanley Cup command and then still a year later ...

Perhaps few low times in Flames' history will match the bitter disappointment of 1988 when, after finishing first overall and getting past the Los Angeles Kings in the opening round of the

Smythe Division playoffs, Calgary was swept by the Oilers. The Flames were called chokers and humiliated in defeat with the long, hot (as in fan/media heat) summer clearly spelling out the consequences of failure to win the big one. People don't remember anything but the last game and nothing is worse for Calgary fans than to lose a final game against Edmonton.

Downplayed through all this is one envious fact: Albertans are fortunate that in the last seven years, either the Oilers or the Flames have been in the Stanley Cup Final and have combined to bring the province five Stanley Cup parades.

True, there may have been some Edmontonians living by ABC hopes (Anybody But Calgary) when the Oilers were eliminated in 1989 by the Kings. However, the reality is that the Edmonton-Calgary hockey rivalry has been great for the fans and produced seven successive Stanley Cup finalists. In today's sports era, where the road to championships is becoming increasingly difficult, the Oiler-Flame feud is based on excellence and respect for the superb job done by each franchise in assembling the right stuff to win.

I remember the 1983 Stanley Cup Final when the Oilers were down three games to none and on the verge of being swept by the Islanders. During the Stanley Cup luncheon, Oilers' coach-general manager-president Glen Sather talked about how his young team sought to emulate the champion Islanders. A year later, the Oilers did just that by dethroning the Islanders.

As Edmonton rose to those heights, the Flames strived for the standard the Oilers set. And now that the Flames hold the bragging rights as champions of 1988-89, the other 20 teams will take aim at them because they now can say they are the best until another team proves otherwise.

It should be noted that in the post-game coverage of the Flames' triumph, Dick Chubey in the *Edmonton Sun* caught up to Sather, who respectfully said: "It takes a hell of an effort to win the Stanley Cup. You don't accomplish what they've achieved by working with mirrors.

"They should be proud; it's something everybody down there should be proud of. It's an accomplishment no one can take away from them … I'm happy for them." When Chubey asked Sather about patronizing the Oilers' most bitter rival, Sather's response was: "When you're a loser, you have to be humble."

Winning the Stanley Cup, as Sather noted, is a rigorous trek. Many pursue, but relatively few achieve. Eleven of the current 21 NHL teams have *never* won a Stanley Cup. What's more unbelievable is that since the NHL's major expansion of 1967 only six franchises have won the Stanley Cup, with three of those six forming dynasties (Montreal, nine wins; Islanders, four wins; Oilers, four wins). The Boston Bruins and the Philadelphia Flyers, each with two wins, and now the Calgary Flames with one victory are the other post-1967 teams with Stanley Cup triumphs.

Of the NHL's original six teams, only one (Montreal) has a Stanley Cup title in the 1980s (over Calgary in 1986), only two won in the 1970s (Montreal in 1971, 1973, 1976, 1977, 1978, 1979; Boston in 1970 and 1972). The Toronto Maple Leafs haven't won the Stanley Cup since 1967; the Chicago Blackhawks not since 1961, when current Flames' goaltending consultant Glenn Hall was their acrobatic Mr. Goalie. The Detroit Red Wings last brought the Stanley Cup to Motor City in 1955, and the Stanley Cup last stayed on Broadway in possession of the New York Rangers in 1940!

The Canadiens of 1988-89 were gunning for that club's 24th Stanley Cup since 1916. Their lineup featured 15 players with Stanley Cup rings, the Flames had none, although head coach Terry Crisp played for the Flyer champions of 1974 and 1975 while assistant coach Doug Risebrough played for the Canadiens' four Stanley Cup winners from 1976 through 1979.

The mission statement by the Flames had been formulated, stressed, and re-emphasized throughout the season and the Stanley Cup drive. Perhaps no one was more certain of the team's conviction than Hakan Loob during a conversation we had at the Los Angeles airport in late January, 1989.

"There is no doubt in my mind that we're going to win the Stanley Cup this year," he said. "We have the team, we have everything – and the players are committed to winning. Montreal does have a good team but they're more defensive-minded. We have more explosive players who can score when we need the goals."

Once the Flames escaped a close series with the Vancouver Canucks, they were, as Crisp would say, breathing new life. They'd dodged the bullet once and intended never to be in such a precarious situation again. As the other series came and went, the Flame snipers did supplement the team's solid defensive play. Even the noted defensive specialists would chip in with timely goals.

"We were destined to go for a Stanley Cup and to win the Stanley Cup and finally we grasped that moment," said goaltender Mike Vernon, unjustly maligned after the Flames' failure in 1988. "It's a great feeling and I guess I can walk around Calgary now with a smile on my face."

The selection of defenceman Al MacInnis for the Conn Smythe Trophy as the most outstanding player in the 1989 playoffs was deserved. However, strong cases for the award were also made for the likes of Doug Gilmour, Joey Mullen, Joel Otto, and Vernon. MacInnis, playing with confidence and shining offensively and defensively, set a record for defencemen with points in 17 consecutive playoff games. His 31 points (seven goals, 24 assists) gave him what no other defenceman – including Bobby Orr, Denis Potvin, Brad Park, Doug Harvey, Paul Coffey, to name a few – had ever achieved, the playoff scoring title.

MacInnis gained nine of his points against the Canadiens (including four goals, two of them game winners) to steer the ship in the Final, while Mullen and Otto came next, each with eight, and Gilmour, seven. Vernon, nothing short of spectacular, and the rest of the lineup were giants, too, but the individual honoured with the individual prize was MacInnis.

"I'd trade the Norris Trophy, the Conn Smythe Trophy, and that (playoff scoring) streak in any day for that Stanley Cup ring," MacInnis said. "Ten or 15 years down the road when I can show all my friends and family the Stanley Cup ring they're going to remember the Calgary Flames and who won the 1989 Stanley Cup at the Montreal Forum. There's not a lot of people who are going to remember the individual awards."

The Calgary Flames' first Stanley Cup will always be treasured as a special time, not only by the people associated with the club and the fans but by myself and my broadcasting partner, Doug Barkley. As a player, Doug was on his way to an outstanding career with the Detroit Red Wings during the 1960s. A no-nonsense, solid defenceman, his NHL days were curtailed by an eye injury and he never played on a Stanley Cup winner despite frequent trips to the Final in his four years with Detroit.

"I was fortunate, or maybe unfortunate is the word, as a player to be in three Finals, but we lost them all," Barkley said. "It's really something … so devastating when you lose. I can just feel for the Calgary players and what it's like to win it."

A tremendous amount of excitement surrounds any organization's climb to the top, and this is felt especially when the club involved is one you follow from day to day. While I never came close to playing on a Stanley Cup winning team, my own meteoric rise to big-league glory having stalled at the Bantam level, the Flames' 1986 trip to the Final was a milestone for me. It is the reverie of every broadcaster in hockey to work a Stanley Cup Final, much as it would be for a baseball broadcaster to work the World Series, a football broadcaster to work (in Canada) the Grey Cup or (in the United States) the Super Bowl, and a basketball broadcaster to work the NBA Championship Series. The fact the Flames in 1986, and again in 1989, found themselves against the Montreal was even more special for me since, as a Maritimer, I was weaned on the Canadiens and the play-by-play of Danny Gallivan.

Broadcasters, like players, have dreams, too. As a youth in my hometown of Campbellton, New Brunswick, I often broadcast aloud as I played our fantasized Stanley Cup Final and the games leading up to it at outdoor rinks or in backyard hockey. You couldn't shut me up inside, either, because that deep-rooted play-by-play broadcasting spilled over to the table hockey I used to play with friends and family.

My hockey career never extended beyond Bantam. I was a goalie and, quite frankly, a fellow named George Berube did me in because no matter how hard I tried my reflexes couldn't react quickly enough to his impressive shot. Having confessed to this, I vehemently deny my nickname was "Sieve"! At this point, I decided to explore other hockey endeavours, which eventually led to my career in broadcasting.

Scott Young, a noted author who created hockey fantasy in a wonderful way with such books as *Scrubs on Skates*, once told a friend of mine that there really isn't much difference in covering hockey at the kids' levels or the pro level. A dressing room is a dressing room, full of little-boy dreams and the desire to win the Stanley Cup.

Throughout my career, I've had the good fortune of being associated with a large number of successful teams. No matter how small-scale those days might seem, in reality they were as important as any Stanley Cup Final for those involved. I can't tell you the thrill it was for me to be the stick boy when the Campbellton Tigers won the New Brunswick/Quebec Senior Hockey League titles in 1962 and 1963. These humble beginnings would eventually lead to the National Hockey League and fulfil for me those rinks of dreams. I was still involved when the Tigers won the North Shore Hockey League and New Brunswick hockey championships in 1965 and also served as assistant manager of Campbellton's provincial champion Midget team in the same year.

Beginning in 1970 I became play-by-play broadcaster of the Tigers on CKNB Radio in Campbellton while serving as the team's general manager. Throughout that time of double duty, the Tigers captured two Hardy Cups (1972 and 1977), emblematic of the Canadian Intermediate hockey championship. In 1978, I broadcast my last hockey game involving the Tigers when they lost the Hardy Cup final to Prince George, British Columbia.

News from Toronto indicated the radio rights of Maple Leaf broadcasts had been up for bids, and the CKO Radio Network out of Toronto gained those rights. I sent in tapes of my work, trusting that the fairness I'd used for my broadcasts back home – along with the quality of the work – would earn me a shot at the big league. I learned a long time ago as I called games featuring the Campbellton Tigers and the Dalhousie Moosehead Rangers – communities separated by 16 miles – that the key to broadcasting is to remember there are two teams on the ice. That training has stuck with me everywhere I have gone.

Well, I got the job as the Maple Leaf broadcaster and, next thing you know, Nancy, Jeff, Trish, and I were on our way to Toronto, Maple Leaf Gardens, and life in the NHL. My first interview would turn out to be Lanny McDonald. And that season, in which the Leafs finished with their last winning record in the past 11 years (34–33–13), included the infamous firing/re-hiring scenario with coach Roger Neilson.

The next season marked the return of Punch Imlach to the Maple Leafs as general manager. This produced one of hockey's biggest trades when, on December 29, 1979, Lanny McDonald was traded to the Colorado Rockies along with Joel Quenneville for Wilf Paiement and Pat Hickey. If you'd told me then that Lanny and I would be reunited in Calgary two years less a month later, I'd have bet anything against it. Funny how things in life work out.

After the 1979-80 season the radio rights went back to CKFH/CJCL in Toronto and I was looking for an NHL broadcasting job once more. I accepted an offer from CHQR in Calgary, which had obtained the radio rights to the Flames, because it afforded the opportunity for me to stay involved at the NHL level. Following the 1979-80 campaign, the Flames had moved to Alberta from Atlanta.

For that first season with the Flames I worked on the broadcast, but from the second season to this day I've been the play-by-play voice, watching the Flames grow into eventual Stanley Cup champions.

I consider myself lucky my hockey path has been filled with such wonderful moments. The Flames' championship season provided another note of personal satisfaction, though it led to probably the most exhaustive day of my broadcasting career. On the day of the third game of the Los Angeles series, we were in Los Angeles for the morning skate while in St. John's, Newfoundland, my son, Jeff, and his Calgary Buffalos were participating in the Air Canada Cup Canadian Midget hockey championship. Despite their 3–2 record in the preliminary round, the Buffalos upset the favoured team from Wexford, Ontario, 5–4, setting the stage for the final between Calgary and Regina, which had won two previous games against Jeff's team during the season.

I'd arranged through Bob Borgen of the Kings and John Shannon of SportsChannel America to pick up the game from St. John's off the CTV telecast in Canada. Scotty Bowman, who was in Los Angeles with *Hockey Night in Canada*, and Cliff Fletcher spent some time watching a nervous me throughout this ordeal, as did some of the Flames' players who were coming off their morning skate.

Wouldn't you know it, Jeff scored Calgary's go-ahead goal, in a fashion reminiscent of Lanny McDonald circling the net and stuffing the puck past the goalie, as the Buffalos won the title, 4–3. Talk about proud, well, Bernie Pascall on CTV mentioned that Jeff was my son and how I was watching out in Los Angeles as I prepared for game three of the Los Angeles-Calgary series. During the post-game celebration, the TV cameras picked up Jeff saying "Hi, Dad!"

Needless to say, the congratulations from the many people associated with the Flames and from others at the Great Western Forum in Los Angeles and Jeff remembering me at a very important moment of his life proved to be too emotional for me. By the time the Flames-Kings game rolled along that Saturday night, I was simply drained ... but proud. Jeff, given little chance to even make his squad because of his size, had achieved his dream. I was about to join Doug Barkley in reporting the Flames' next step en route to their quest.

Thirty-two days later, the Flames completed their task, touching off a massive party on downtown Calgary's Electric Avenue as thousands spilled into the streets.

At the end of that decisive game, I had a feeling of disbelief ... stunned, really, that the Flames had won the Stanley Cup. After all the years of the team climbing the mountain, it had now reached the peak and planted the flaming "C" as testimony to the conquest.

They had become The Eternal Flames.

Hip, hip, hooray . . . Mike Vernon jumps for joy as the final buzzer sounds and the Flames win the Stanley Cup. *(Calgary Sun photo)*

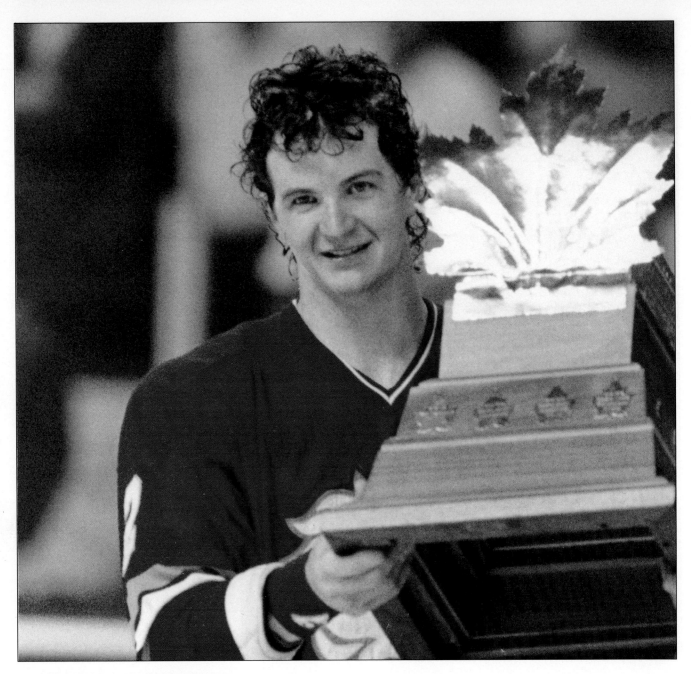

The MVP . . . Flames' defenceman Al MacInnis, the first
defenceman to win a playoff
scoring title, which included a
record for defencemen with a
17-game playoff scoring streak,
hoists the Conn Smythe Trophy
he won as most outstanding
player in the 1989 playoffs.
(Calgary Sun photo)

Above: Al's shot is a blast . . . Montreal goalie Patrick Roy had more than enough of the bullet drives by the Flames' Al MacInnis. Here, Joel Otto and Doug Gilmour whoop it up after MacInnis's howitzer from the point registered Calgary's first goal of the Final series. The Flames went on to win the game, 3–2, with two goals from MacInnis. *(Calgary Sun photo)*

Inset: Different points of view . . . Doug Gilmour and Montreal's Bobby Smith take part in a verbal exchange in front of referee Andy van Hellemond. *(Calgary Sun photo)*

Oh no, not again! . . . Patrick Roy
watches helplessly as Al MacInnis
completes a three-on-one with
Joel Otto and Lanny McDonald
(seen here at the Montreal
doorstep) with his second goal in
less than two minutes during
Game 1. Theoren Fleury's second-
period goal would give Calgary
the victory. *(Calgary Sun photo)*

Razor sharp . . . Mike Vernon's strong play permitted the Flames to weather the early Montreal storm and surge to the 4–2 win in Game 6. *(Calgary Sun photo)*

Habs are down . . . Jamie Macoun's check on Bob Gainey put the Montreal captain on the ice and dislodged his helmet. Calgary's 3–2 triumph in Game 5 at home set the stage for Montreal's elimination two nights later. *(Calgary Sun photo)*

Above: Always around the net . . . Joey Mullen, ever dangerous, didn't score on this play on Patrick Roy's doorstep but he led Flame scorers in the Final against Montreal with five goals.
(*Calgary Sun photo*)

Inset: Tête-à-tête . . . Montreal's Chris Chelios and Calgary's Rob Ramage exchange unpleasantries while the Flames' Colin Patterson arrives to restrain his teammate.
(*Calgary Sun photo*)

Top Right: Key goal . . . Doug Gilmour, along with Joey Mullen and Joel Otto, celebrates his goal during the second period of pivotal Game 4 in Montreal, a 4–2 win. *(Calgary Sun photo)*

Bottom: Only seconds to go . . . The clock kept ticking and the hoopla kept growing at the Flames' bench in those final few seconds. Trainer Bearcat Murray watches as the emotion grips Dana Murzyn (5), Ric Nattress (6), Brad McCrimmon (4), Lanny McDonald (9), Joe Nieuwendyk (25), Colin Patterson (11), Mark Hunter (22), Theoren Fleury (14), and equipment manager Bobby Stewart. *(Calgary Sun photo)*

Embraceable Flames . . . Assistant coach Tom Watt, Theoren Fleury, and others capture the moment of Stanley Cup triumph with this show of emotion. *(Calgary Sun photo)*

Above: A kiss for luck . . . Flames' forward Jiri Hrdina relishes his finest moment in the NHL as he plants a kiss on the Stanley Cup during the postgame skate with his mates around the Montreal Forum ice. Al MacInnis (2) looks on. *(Calgary Sun photo)*

Inset: Wow, look at all those names . . . Flames' head coach Terry Crisp marvels at the names on the Stanley Cup. His is there as a player (Philadelphia in 1974 and 1975). Now it'll go on as a coach. *(Calgary Sun photo)*

Who Are These Guys, Anyway?

Putting together a winning combination is much like fitting the pieces to a jigsaw puzzle. No other organization in the history of the National Hockey League reflects a better knack at this than the Montreal Canadiens.

Montreal-born Cliff Fletcher is a disciple of the Canadiens' system, after serving his apprenticeship in a variety of capacities in the Canadiens' development system under the tutelage of the renowned genius, Sam Pollock. Known as hockey's Godfather, Pollock masterminded some memorable swaps, including one in which he pried away California's first-round draft pick in 1971 and Francois Lacombe during a trade in May, 1970, as the Golden Seals received Ernie Hicke and Montreal's first-round pick in 1970. Lacombe was by no means the key in the transaction.

Pollock converted that No. 1 overall pick to pluck future Hall-of-Famer Guy Lafleur from the Quebec Remparts. Through master planning such as that, Pollock was a winner at every level in hockey, including the NHL, with nine Stanley Cups in 14 years as general manager of the Canadiens.

NHL expansion opened the doors for more employment at all hockey levels and brought upcoming administrators to the front much more rapidly than the original six teams could ever do. Fletcher was among this group of young and eager executive material seeking to climb that ladder hoping for success. In 1967, he became eastern Canada scout for the St. Louis Blues, eventually rising to assistant general manager for the Blues in 1969. Around the same time, another Montrealer and a good friend of Fletcher's, Bill Torrey, received his indoctrination with the California Seals. When the NHL expanded by two teams for the

1972-73 season, Torrey accepted the post as general manager of the New York Islanders while Fletcher assumed the same position with the Atlanta Flames.

To this day, each holds the GM's title with the same organization and each now has Stanley Cup-winning credentials! The modus operandi for both franchises has stressed stability and leadership from the general manager, building via the draft sprinkled with sharp trades, and occasional valuable free-agent acquisitions.

The expansion Blues, with Glenn Hall and Jacques Plante as goaltenders, reached the NHL finals from 1968 through 1970, losing the Stanley Cup twice to Montreal and once to Boston. Clearly, Fletcher had established himself as one of the most astute youthful hockey executives and was prepared to operate his own franchise when he signed with the Flames on January 10, 1972.

The Flames debuted on the ice that fall with Bernie (Boom Boom) Geoffrion, the former Canadiens' great, behind the bench. In 17 years with the Flames, Fletcher's teams have only missed the playoffs twice and not since 1975. Given the enormous workload of selling hockey in Georgia, it's a credit Fletcher's Atlanta Flames compiled a winning percentage (268 wins, 260 losses, 108 ties), and the fans were loyal but too few to salvage the franchise. The warm weather also made it difficult for fans and for players to think hockey.

Due to the pressure of winning immediately, his building of the Flames initially took the route of veteran players. But when the franchise moved to Calgary under sound ownership and a solid hockey environment, he was able to retain and develop draft picks, sign key free agents, and generate vital trades in exchange for the pool of talent he'd cultivated in the process.

The positive impact of the move to Calgary was instantaneous, as the Flames produced their best season (to that point) in 1980-81 with 92 points and a meteoric blast-off in the playoffs in which they reached the semifinals. Until that season, the Flames were noted playoff busts in Atlanta, losing all six series, winning only two of 17 playoff games, and being out-scored 62–32.

The Flames have made Calgary miserable for visitors right from the outset when they were 25–5–10 at the old Corral, a standard only eclipsed in 1988-89 when they had the finest home record in the NHL, 32–4–4 at the Olympic Saddledome. At Calgary, they have posted 363 wins, 256 losses, and 101 ties for a .574 winning percentage. Their playoff mark, 16–6 in 1989, now stands at 55–49 for a .529 winning percentage, a vast difference from the .118 playoff percentage experienced through those nightmarish Atlanta failures.

The Flames are a beacon of strength in the NHL and no one reflects that image more than Fletcher. He has always surrounded himself with a loyal staff that, in turn, has his utmost support.

He is a classy individual who cares about the well-being of his players, his coaches, his assistants, all staffers, and their families. Terry Crisp is only the fifth coach in Flames' history and, as he and assistants Doug Risebrough and Tom Watt steered the Flames toward their moment of glory in 1989, Fletcher remembered the past by inviting previous head coaches to Calgary during the Final. After all, they were part of shaping the Flames of '89.

Fred Creighton, 1974 through 1979, and Bob Johnson, 1982 through 1987, were able to attend; Geoffrion, who coached the Flames for just over two seasons, was unable to attend the first part of the Final and said he could be counted on if a seventh game was necessary. It wasn't, of course, but Boom Boom let me know on a pre-game show that while he was in Atlanta, his heart was in Calgary with the Flames.

Al MacNeil, the Flames' head coach from 1979-80 through 1981-82, was already in Calgary in his capacity as assistant general manager to Fletcher. Recently, he was promoted to vice-president, hockey operations. Al, who was an assistant coach for the Team Canada club Fletcher put together in 1981, is another ex-Canadien and was the skipper of Montreal's 1971 Stanley Cup winner.

Fletcher takes pride in running a first-rate operation. I have never heard a Flame player, present or past, complain about the treatment received from the Flames. Lanny McDonald's wife, Ardell, called Cliff on the day of Game 5 against Montreal to ask if there were plans for the Flame wives and girlfriends to travel to Montreal for Game 6. Her intention was to complete baby-sitting plans should the voyage take place. "There was no hesitation on Cliff's part so I think the reservations were made before I called," Ardell said. "That was really a generous offer by Cliff and the owners to take us. When I asked Cliff if it depended on us winning the game that night, he said, 'Well, number one, we're not going to lose, we are going to win tonight, and if there's a chance we're not going to win tonight, I'm still going to take you.' "

The Flames' interest in the well-being of the players includes retention of two part-time psychologists, Max Offenberger and Hap Davis. Max, who resides in the Boston area and helped in the rehabilitation of former Bruin Derek Sanderson, supplies additional culinary expertise since he's noted for advising the players of the finer restaurants on the circuit.

The community spirit the Flames exude begins right with the club owners, Norman Green, Harley Hotchkiss, Norman Kwong,

Sonia Scurfield, Byron Seaman, and Daryl Seaman. It's been a plus to Cliff Fletcher that the six owners let him run the operation without interference and with one goal in mind: provide Calgarians with a club they can take pride in. Many of the profits from the Flames' operation go back to amateur hockey in Canada through Hockey Canada. The club is totally supportive of Canada's international hockey program and even loaned Jim Peplinski and Brian Bradley to the Canadian Olympic team for the 1988 Winter Games.

Fletcher remains close to the scouting ranks by bird-dogging prospects whenever he can, either in North America or Europe. The Flames have an extensive scouting staff, which includes chief scout Gerry Blair, co-ordinator of scouting Ian McKenzie, and scouts Al Godfrey, Larry Popein, Gerry McNamara, Ray Clearwater, Lou Reycroft, Ben Hays, Garth Malarchuk, David Mayville, Lars Norman, Tom Thompson, and Bill White. MacNeil provides additional scouting support at all levels, including advance scouting of upcoming opponents or of players the Flames are interested in pursuing via the trade route.

Al Coates, assistant to the president, is another key component of the Flames' day-to-day operation. While he has a wide area of duties, Coates also co-ordinates all aspects pertaining to travel, knowing that foul-ups in this area can disrupt the team's concentration on winning. Considering the Flames' 1989 schedule of 113 games, 103 practices (some of which were optional), 76 trips for about 80,185 air miles, seven bus trips from one game site to another, and 86 nights spread across 27 hotels, one can appreciate the burden on Coates and executive secretary June Yeates to ensure pre-trip arrangements are followed through.

An interesting aspect of Fletcher's post-Cup comments was his instant mention of the Flame family and the immediate staff. "I'm so proud of every one in the organization," he said, "Coatsy (Al Coates) and Al MacNeil, who have to put up with my guff on a daily basis, and, of course, the scouting staff. If you go back and analyse the draft since 1980 and where we've been drafting, Gerry Blair, Ian McKenzie, and their staff have done a job second to none. They're the main reason we're looking good here tonight."

During the 1989 playoffs, the Flames unveiled a unique scouting system in which they sent Popein and McNamara together to scout potential opponents. On one night, Popein would scout one team and McNamara the other before comparing notes the next day. For the following game, each would isolate on the other team and, once more, huddle for analyses. They believed the concentration on one team by one man, rather than two teams by one man, provided in-depth previews of upcoming foes.

The men behind the Flames' bench, head coach Terry Crisp and assistants Tom Watt and Doug Risebrough, are not strangers to winning ways since Crisp and Risebrough celebrated Cup wins as players and Tom, a former NHL coach of the year at Winnipeg, became a legend while coaching the University of Toronto Blues.

The three-man system worked well, with Crisp giving Watt and Risebrough major duties while not interfering. Risebrough and Watt would alternate behind the Flames' bench with Crisp (the one not behind the bench would be in the press box with a headset connection to the other). There were some exceptions to the rotation in the regular season because Tom would be behind the bench for games against his former teams (Winnipeg and Vancouver) while Doug would get the call when the Flames played Montreal.

When Crisp assumed the head coaching duties in May, 1987, his first comment was: "I am not Bob Johnson." A winner at every level he has coached, Crisp's two-year regular-season mark with the Flames is 102 wins, 40 losses, and 18 ties for a phenomenal .694 percentage. He has won 100 career games faster than any other coach in league history and now has a career playoff record of 20 victories and 11 losses (.645 percentage).

Risebrough, a fiery competitor through 13 NHL seasons with Montreal and Calgary, joined the coaching ranks for the 1987-88 season after injuries finally took their toll. He often played in pain and, while he didn't possess the greatest talent in the world, he played with outstanding determination. Certainly, anyone who saw him perform never felt cheated, and I have never met anyone who hated to lose or took losses as hard as Doug. Obtaining Doug Risebrough from Montreal and the trade that brought Lanny McDonald from Colorado were factors that taught the Flames how to win. It was not surprising that Risebrough, in charge of the Flames' penalty killing, prepared it to be the best in the NHL, with an 82.9 per cent efficiency rating in 1989. Many factors, of course, contributed to the Flames' victory over Montreal, but consider this: in the three games played at Montreal in the Final, the Flames did not permit a goal in 18 Canadiens' power play opportunities! ties!

Risebrough showed managerial skills and inclination, so it came as no surprise when, on June 26, the Flames' restructuring elevated Doug to assistant general manager. Crisp, rewarded with a new three-year contract, then upgraded former Flame Paul Baxter from the farm team at Salt Lake City to join Watt in the roles as assistants.

While Crisp and Risebrough were emotional types, Watt, by contrast, brought cooler mannerisms to go along with his wealth of NHL coaching experience with the Canucks and the Jets. Watt replaced Pierre Page, who had left the Flames to accept the head coaching position with the Minnesota North Stars. At the outset Watt revealed an additional reason why it was imperative for the Flames to win in 1989: "My daughter's getting married this summer and I need the bonus money to pay for the wedding."

Watt and Risebrough joined Crisp in making decisions by committee, and no other issue became tougher than deciding on scratches from a roster full of character players who wanted to do virtually anything to win. "It's not easy telling the type of players we have that they're not going to play," Crisp said.

In fact, for Crisp the most anguish he's ever endured as a head coach occurred before Game 6 versus Montreal. The final decision was to play Lanny McDonald and sit out Jim Peplinski and Tim Hunter. McDonald, who'd missed the three previous games, scored a key go-ahead goal, making it look like the right move. But throughout the ordeal, Crisp related to Peplinski and Tim Hunter. In 1975 when the Flyers won their second consecutive Stanley Cup, in Buffalo, Philadelphia coach Fred Shero scratched a player named Terry Crisp from the lineup. The hurt Crisp felt was consoled by the fact the Flyers won the Stanley Cup, and that's all that really mattered.

The Flames, to their credit, have assembled a roster so deep in talent it is envied. On the day of the fourth game of the Smythe Division final against Los Angeles, Roger Neilson, a fine coach and a keen judge of talent as a scout for the Chicago Blackhawks, described the Flames' profound organization.

"They're doing very well in the playoffs right now and their future looks very, very good," said the man known as Captain Video. "I did a little bit of research earlier in the season and came away with the conclusion the Flames, ahead of any NHL team, had more NHL prospects in their system, either playing in the NHL or in their farm system, with the ability to play in the NHL." He noted the strength in the fact at least seven players at the Flames' Salt Lake City affiliate plus several others playing at the Junior and college levels were, in his view, bonafide NHLers.

Fletcher and his staff crafted the Flames by wise picks in the amateur draft, some good free agent acquisitions, and several shrewd trades. Thus was created the Calgary Stanley Cup winners.

The Amateur Draft Picks

THEOREN FLEURY – #14. Centre, eighth-round selection (166th overall) 1987 draft from the Moose Jaw Warriors. Nicknames: Theo or Weasel. Age at Stanley Cup win: 20. At 5-foot-6, 155 pounds, this Michael J. Fox look-alike plays like he's 6-foot-6, 255 pounds. He's an agitator, darting, dashing, and dangerous. Glenn Hall predicts he's destined to hit the 50-goal-a-season plateau. A scorer at all levels of hockey, he gained promotion from Salt Lake City on January 1, 1989, intending to stay in the NHL. He did. He certainly adjusted to the good-natured needling regarding his size. Ric Nattress on one occasion called Theoren the second team mascot, along with the real mascot, Harvey the Hound.

JIRI HRDINA – #17. Centre/wing, eighth-round selection (159th overall) 1984 draft from Sparta Prava (Czechoslovakia). Nicknames: George or Jir-she. Age at Stanley Cup win: 31. The 6-foot 195-pounder is a fun-loving individual who can hit, skate, and score. A premier player with the Czechoslovakian national team, he represented his country at the '88 Olympic Winter Games in Calgary, then made his Flames' start on March 3, 1988.

TIM HUNTER – #19. Co-Captain. Right wing, third-round selection (54th overall) 1979 draft from the Seattle Breakers. Nickname: Hunts. Age at Stanley Cup win: 28. A leader. The 6-foot-2, 202-pounder is tough on the ice but disciplined. Off the ice, he's a gentleman noted for his public speaking and charitable work. The Flames' all-time penalty leader began as a defenceman but was moved to right wing by then coach Badger Bob Johnson. Set the Flame penalty-minute record (371) in 1988-89.

HAKAN LOOB – #12. Right wing, ninth-round selection (181st overall) 1980 draft from Farjestads BK (Sweden). Nicknames: Loober or Loobin. Age at Stanley Cup win: 28. Nifty. The 5-foot-9, 175-pounder joined the Flames in 1983 and became the first Swedish-born player to score 50 goals in a season (1987-88). He is the first Flame ever voted to the NHL First All-Star team (1987-88). His only regret was never playing in an NHL All-Star game. The Stanley Cup ended a great year for him as he ended his NHL career and returned to Sweden due to family reasons. The chants of "Loob! Loob! Loob!" will be missed at the Saddledome.

AL MACINNIS – #2. Defenceman, first-round selection (15th overall) 1981 draft from the Kitchener Rangers. Nickname: Chopper. Age at Stanley Cup win: 25. Rocket shot. Rapid growth defensively to go along with superb offensive ability. Master at dumping puck out of own zone to relieve pressure with slow-moving flip shot. (It almost looks like the puck will stop in mid-air.) MacInnis, at 6-foot-2, 196 pounds, has developed into one of NHL's elite defencemen and definite Norris Trophy candidate. His progress became evident throughout the playoffs as he provided leadership and key goals.

JOE NIEUWENDYK – #25. Centre, second-round selection (27th overall, obtained along with a second-round draft pick, Stephane Matteau, from Minnesota for Kent Nilsson in trade of June 15, 1985) from Cornell University. Nickname: Nieuwy. Age at Stanley Cup win: 22. Hands. Instinct. Guts. Natural goal scorer. Scored 51 goals in each of his first two NHL seasons (and led Flame scorers in game-winning goals each season, eight in 1987-88 and 11 in 1988-89). The 6-foot-1, 175-pounder takes a physical beating but never quits until he beats you on the scoreboard. Good needler. Likes to tell story of how he and Lanny McDonald went to Children's Hospital last Christmas Eve to visit youngsters and one of the nurses said: "Gee, Lanny, it's nice of you to bring your son with you."

JIM PEPLINSKI – #24. Co-Captain. Left wing, fourth-round selection (75th overall) 1979 draft from the Toronto Marlboros. Nicknames: Pep or Pepper. Age at Stanley Cup win: 28. Hard-nosed. Sincere. A clown when he wants to liven things up. No other Flame has played more games (699 regular season; 99 play-offs). Peplinski (6-foot-3, 209 pounds) joined the Flames when they came to Calgary and is a solid leader on and off the ice. Set up one of the most important, if not the most vital, goals in Flames' history when his goalmouth pass enabled Joel Otto to sink the Canucks in seventh game overtime.

SERGEI PRIAKIN – #16. Left wing, 12th-round selection (252nd overall) 1988 draft from Wings of the Soviet (Soviet Union). Nickname: They'll have to think of one. Age at Stanley Cup win: 25. The Flames became the first NHL team to receive permission from the Soviet Ice Hockey Federation to sign a Soviet player when they inked the captain of the Soviet Wings to a contract on March 29, 1989. At the time of the signing, Cliff Fletcher made it quite clear that Sergei was not being signed as a saviour for the 1988-89 playoffs. That word was kept as Sergei played only two regular-season and one playoff games.

GARY ROBERTS – #10. Left wing, first-round selection (12th overall) 1984 draft from the Guelph Platers. Nickname: Robs. Age at Stanley Cup win: 23. Dogged determination. Tough checker and ideal corner man. Played on Memorial Cup winners with Guelph (where he was captain) and Ottawa. Played minor hockey in Whitby-Oshawa area with Joe Nieuwendyk and, in storybook fashion, they are linemates with Calgary. Roberts, 6-foot-1, 190 pounds, plays a rugged game. While he and Nieuwendyk are close friends (Joe was Gary's best man for Roberts's off-season wedding) they did have a spirited fight during last year's training camp.

GARY SUTER – #20. Defenceman, ninth-round selection (180th overall) 1984 draft from the University of Wisconsin. Nickname: Suits. Age at Stanley Cup win: 24. Great talent. This 6-foot, 190-pounder is a hard-luck guy as injuries limited his playoff time in each of Calgary's Final appearances. An appendectomy kept him out of 16 games in February-March and, once he'd returned to the lineup, a broken jaw in the Vancouver series sidelined him for the rest of the playoffs.

MIKE VERNON – #30. Goaltender, third-round selection (56th overall) 1981 draft from the Calgary Wranglers. Nicknames: Vernie or Mikey. Age at Stanley Cup win: 26. At 5-foot-9, 155 pounds, he's quick as a cat. Great glove hand although his toe save on Petri Skriko stood out like, well, a sore thumb! It was the Flames' salvation. Proved to his critics that he not only can be a clutch goalie but he is a great goalie. The heat was on him in 1988-89 after he was unduly blamed for Calgary's 1988 loss to Edmonton. He was outstanding in 1989.

The Free Agent Signings

JAMIE MACOUN – #34. Defenceman, signed January 30, 1983, from Ohio State University. Nickname: Cooner. Age at Stanley Cup win: 27. Mr. Comeback. He was fortunate to be alive following a car accident (May, 1987). Given a slim chance of ever playing hockey again after suffering severe nerve damage to his left arm, he was determined to return before the end of the 1987-88 season. The return was postponed until last season when he suited up for 72 regular-season games and all the playoff games. While persevering and dedicating himself to getting back to help the Flames win a Stanley Cup, the 6-foot-2, 197-pounder endured another hardship as his mother died early into the 1988-89 season. An incredible story about a very determined individual.

JOEL OTTO – #29. Centre, signed September 11, 1984, from Bemidji State. Nickname: Otts. Age at Stanley Cup win: 27.

Intense. Helmet-to-helmet face-off man. Soft skate blade. Hard hands. Power-play contributor. Much sought by other clubs in trade talks with the Flames, this 6-foot-4, 220-pounder is a staunch competitor and one of the top defensive centres in the NHL. He also finds ways of producing key offensive results as proven by his 10 power-play goals during the regular season and 19 points in 22 playoff games, including that all-essential overtime winner off his skate against Vancouver.

COLIN PATTERSON – #11. Right/left wing, signed March 24, 1983, from Clarkson College. Nicknames: Patter or Heater. Age at Stanley Cup win: 29. The NHL's Rodney Dangerfield in that he doesn't get much respect for his superb defensive work. He doesn't even have a bubble-gum card yet after six solid seasons. But that's changing. He and his Hespeler stick scored a key goal in the decisive game and, as Gary Suter said, "Colin Patterson is as smooth as Selke," in reference to Colin gaining more and more recognition for the Frank Selke Trophy awarded to the NHL's top defensive forward. He finished second to Montreal's Guy Carbonneau in the 1989 Selke voting.

The Trade Acquisitions

DOUG GILMOUR – #39. Centre, acquired from the St. Louis Blues along with Steve Bozek, Michael Dark, and Mark Hunter for Mike Bullard, Tim Corkery, and Craig Coxe on September 5, 1988. Nickname: Killer. Age at Stanley Cup win: 25. A sniper with a definite killer instinct. Showed tremendous grace under personal pressure in 1988-89 and, after what he termed a sub-par performance in the Vancouver series, he bounced back to shine en route to the Stanley Cup win. The 5-foot-11, 165-pounder endured a traumatic season combining frequent legal and grand jury appointments in St. Louis with the Flames' schedule. On December 27, 1988, Gilmour, his family, and friends got the best Christmas present possible when a St. Louis grand jury decided not to indict Gilmour on charges related to alleged sexual misconduct with a 14-year-old girl. The bizarre case, which became public only days before the Blues traded him to Calgary, could have ruined not only Gilmour's career but his personal life. Instead, given the support from his wife Robyne, family, friends, and the Flames, he handled the situation with class, stating his innocence would be proven in due course. "I couldn't understand why it happened," he said. "All I could do was be strong, play hockey, and prove to everybody, including myself, that this shouldn't have been there." Gilmour, a standout in the 1987 Canada Cup and a thorn in the side of all rivals while in St. Louis, was just as intense with the Flames, solidifying his rank as one of the best centres in hockey today.

MARK HUNTER – #22. Right wing, acquired from the St. Louis Blues along with Steve Bozek, Michael Dark, and Doug Gilmour for Mike Bullard, Tim Corkery, and Craig Coxe on September 5, 1988. Nickname: Gus. Age at Stanley Cup win: 25. Rugged, hard-nosed, and a hitter (6-foot, 190 pounds) who comes from a family that produced other prominent scrappy NHLers in brothers Dave and Dale. Hall-of-Famer Bert Olmstead, a hard-nosed player in his career, travelled with the Flames during the Final and noted Calgary received a psychological lift and physical presence with Hunter in the lineup. The Flames sought him for his toughness and potential 30-40 goals but injuries limited him to 22. The penalty call against him in the second overtime in game three versus Montreal turned the Final series around for Calgary. Winning the Stanley Cup was sweet for Mark since he donned the Canadiens' colours after they chose him in the first round (seventh overall) of the 1981 Draft.

BRIAN MACLELLAN – #27. Left wing, acquired from the Minnesota North Stars along with either Minnesota's fourth-round draft pick in 1989 or 1990 for popular Perry Berezan and Shane Churla on March 4, 1989. Nickname: Big Mac. Age at Stanley Cup win: 30. Physical and the big winger (6-foot-3, 215 pounds) the Flames sought for the stretch run. He felt the more ice time he received, the better he played. MacLellan did exactly what the Flames expected of him through the final games of the regular season and the playoffs.

BRAD McCRIMMON – #4. Defenceman, acquired from the Philadelphia Flyers for a third-round draft choice in 1988 and a first-round draft choice in 1989 (subsequently traded to Toronto) on August 26, 1987. Nicknames: Sarge or Beast. Age at Stanley Cup win: 30. Takes charge. Stands guard in front of the net. When the Flames acquired the 5-foot-11, 197-pounder, for what they gave up they had to win the Stanley Cup to justify the deal. Well, they didn't win in the first year, through no fault of Brad's, who won the Emery Edge Award with the best plus (+48) in the NHL. Last year, he was tied for fourth (+43) and, once more, was a leader toward that championship season.

LANNY MCDONALD – #9. Co-Captain. Right wing, acquired from the Colorado Rockies along with a fourth-round 1983 draft choice (subsequently transferred to the New York Islanders) for Don Lever and Bob MacMillan on November 25, 1981. Nicknames: Mac or Larry. Age at Stanley Cup win: 36. Finally, the miracle for the classy guy. A champion in the truest sense of the word who put his 6-foot, 194-pound body on the line throughout his career and used his community spirit off the ice to assist worthwhile causes such as the Canadian Special Olympics. With his Yosemite Sam moustache, outstanding personality, and constant giving of himself to the other players, to the fans, and to the media, he has been a tremendous ambassador for hockey and for Canada. There's no doubt he will be in the Hockey Hall of Fame as soon as he is eligible. He deserves it.

JOEY MULLEN – #7. Right wing, acquired from the St. Louis Blues along with Terry Johnson and Rik Wilson for Eddy Beers, Charlie Bourgeois, and Gino Cavallini on February 1, 1986. Nicknames: Mully or Sch-mo. Age at Stanley Cup win: 32. "Go ahead, hit me again … I'll get my revenge the only way I know how and that's to put points on the board." That's the way the 5-foot-9, 180-pound Mullen operates. He takes a beating but keeps on scoring to the point where last season he set a record for most points (110) by an American-born player. He led the Flames in points and tied with Joe Nieuwendyk for most goals (51). Then, in the playoffs, he led all playoff scorers with 16 goals. An amazing story, he came out of the tough Hell's Kitchen area of New York City to star in the NHL. Very close to Lanny McDonald; the two roomed together for several seasons. Quiet and humble – the two words he most often uses are: "Thank you." Sometimes that's his entire speech when accepting one of his many Molson Cup awards.

DANA MURZYN – #5. Defenceman, acquired from the Hartford Whalers along with Shane Churla for Lane MacDonald, Neil Sheehy, and Carey Wilson on January 3, 1988. Nickname: Duke. Age at Stanley Cup win: 22. Gained tremendous confidence when given regular duty and formed quite a tandem with Al MacInnis. In a strange twist of fate, the Flames intended to select Murzyn in the first round of the 1985 draft but the Whalers, choosing ahead of Calgary, made the former Calgary Wrangler their pick (fifth overall). He has developed into a very steady blueliner and, with his 6-foot-2, 200-pound frame, he keeps the front of the net clear for his goaltenders. His skating advanced last season following the power-skating lessons he took in the summer of '88.

RIC NATTRESS – #6. Defenceman, acquired from the St. Louis Blues for a fourth-round choice in the 1987 draft and a fifth-round choice in the 1988 draft on June 13, 1987. Nicknames: Nats or Natter. Age at Stanley Cup win (in fact, it was his birthday): 27. Coming through when called on, he went from being press-box custodian, so to speak, as he played in only 38 regular-season games, to become a steadying influence on the blueline in 19 play-off games. During the 1986 Campbell Conference final, players such as Nattress and Doug Gilmour stood out for the Blues against the Flames. He was obtained to assist a defence decimated by injuries and retirements in 1987. The 6-foot-2, 210-pounder played solidly in the 1989 playoffs.

ROB RAMAGE – #55. Defenceman, acquired from the St. Louis Blues along with goaltender Rick Wamsley for Steve Bozek and Brett Hull on March 8, 1988. Nickname: Rammer. Age at Stanley Cup win: 30. While his workload was significantly reduced from his days at St. Louis, like Ric Nattress, when Ramage was called into action he became a positive force. When Gary Suter was side-lined, Rob not only provided defensive assistance but filled the point position on the power play extremely well. The 6-foot-2, 195-pounder became a steadying influence for the younger players on the team. The Flames traded Ramage to Toronto for a 1989 second-round draft pick and selected left winger Kent Manderville 24th overall. They're hoping history will repeat itself since Manderville, picked three spots higher than Nieuwendyk, will attend Joe's alma mater (Cornell University).

RICK WAMSLEY – #31. Goaltender, acquired from the St. Louis Blues along with Rob Ramage for Steve Bozek and Brett Hull on March 8, 1988. Nicknames: Wammer or Big Tub of Goo. Age at Stanley Cup win (like Nattress, his birthday): 30. An excellent team player who provides some great one-liners. He never grumbled even with Mike Vernon getting the majority of assignments late in the season and throughout the playoffs. Rick keeps his team up at all times and often sits down with Vernon to discuss shooters. When called on, Rick turned in some spectacular performances, in fact, he posted Calgary's only two shutouts during the regular season. One time in Detroit last season with the Flames running away, a fan near the Calgary bench yelled out: "Hey, Wamsley, if you were playing tonight, the Red Wings would be ahead 7–1!" To which Wamsley, in his fine humour, replied: "No, but it might be 7–7!"

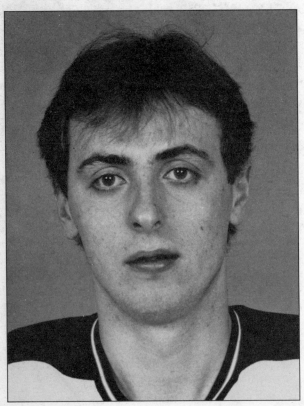

Top Left: Brian MacLellan
Top Right: Rick Wamsley
Left: Sergei Priakin

Top Left: Theoren Fleury
Top Right: Joel Otto
Right: Mark Hunter

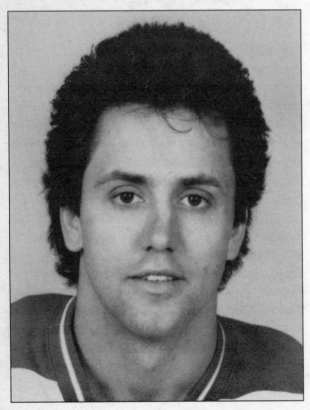

Top Left: Joe Nieuwendyk
Top Right: Mike Vernon
Left: Doug Gilmour

Top Left: Al MacInnis
Top Right: Tim Hunter
Right: Dana Murzyn

Top Left: Brad McCrimmon
Top Right: Jamie Macoun
Left: Gary Suter

Top Left: Rob Ramage
Top Right: Ric Nattress
Right: Colin Patterson

Top Left: Gary Roberts
Top Right: Joe Mullen
Left: Jiri Hrdina

Top Left: Hakan Loob
Top Right: Jim Peplinski
Right: Lanny McDonald

Top Left: Al Coates
Bottom Left: Cliff Fletcher

Top Middle: Terry Crisp
Bottom Middle: Doug Risebrough

Top Right: Al MacNeil
Bottom Right: Tom Watt

Regaining Respect

**he distress and misery** the Calgary Flames endured just one year ago seems to have faded into the distant past. They had been assailed not only for losing the Smythe Division final to the hated Edmonton Oilers but for bowing out of the playoffs with four straight losses. Winning the Presidents' Trophy in 1987-88 with 105 points was no big deal because, in the end, the Stanley Cup dream had gotten away ... again. The bandwagon, unable to accommodate the passengers along the ride to the 1986 Stanley Cup Final, became short of supporters thanks to playoff failures in the first round (to Winnipeg) in 1987 and in the second round (to Edmonton) in 1988.

Answering the sceptics could be done in only one way – by capturing the Stanley Cup. Then, and only then, would the Flames erase the images from the haunting past.

"A lot of people were wondering why we went out in four straight to the Oilers," Al MacInnis would tell me. "In the game of sports, you don't have those answers. But we knew, once training camp started, we talked about defence and making the commitment where we had 25 guys put aside the personal goals. Everybody was hungry; everybody wanted the same thing and that was the Stanley Cup."

The 1988-89 NHL season created more interest than any prior season. The August 9, 1988, trade – the greatest deal in the history of hockey and, arguably, all of professional sports – shocked everyone as Wayne Gretzky, Mike Krushelnyski, and Marty McSorley were shipped to the Los Angeles Kings for Jimmy Carson, Martin Gelinas, Los Angeles's first-round draft choices in 1989, 1991, and 1993, plus a reported $15 million.

On the Pat Sajak show in late July of this year, Kings' owner Bruce McNall said the entire Gretzky package cost about $40 million. McNall told Sajak and the national television audience he thought at the time of the transaction it might take eight years to pay for that trade. But one year after buying the Kings for $20 million the well-respected and gracious McNall revealed he's now receiving offers in the $80-million to $100-million range!

McNall wants the Stanley Cup for the Kings and no move stressed this more than the Great Gretzky Gain. Gretzky brought credibility to the Kings, who suddenly were elevated to Stanley Cup contenders. The Oilers were still laden with talent while the Vancouver Canucks and the Winnipeg Jets believed they'd strengthened themselves. The Smythe Division race, then, promised to be tight and exciting, and was expected to produce the Clarence Campbell Conference champion to challenge for the Stanley Cup.

Sceptics may have questioned whether the Flames had the chemistry and character to maximize their ample ability, but one who believed right from the start was Wayne Gretzky. On the morning of the Flames' second game of the season, I chatted with Gretzky at the Great Western Forum in Inglewood, California. "You know, the Flames made themselves a heck of a deal getting Doug Gilmour from St. Louis," Gretzky said. "In my opinion, he is among the top five centres in the league." Then, he added that Mike Vernon was among the best goaltenders in the NHL and predicted an outstanding season for him.

When Wayne Gretzky speaks, one has to listen. Based on his early-season prognostications, the reference "Great One" is not confined to his ability as a hockey player. The man knows his stuff and, indeed, Gilmour and Vernon became two stars in what became the championship season.

Gretzky became quite familiar with Gilmour's prowess during the Canada Cup of 1987. While Mario Lemieux and Gretzky looked after Team Canada's artillery, Gilmour, a noted scorer, caught everyone's attention with standout defensive play. Gilmour and Gretzky became quite close friends and when Wayne would visit then fiancée Janet Jones in St. Louis, they would occasionally get together with Doug and his wife, Robyne.

As for Vernon, well, he did post a 9–5–2 lifetime regular-season record against the Oilers in the Gretzky years. That impressive total is overshadowed by the overtime goal Gretzky fired high over Vernon's glove hand in the second game of the '88 Edmonton sweep. That goal was replayed in the opening of every *Hockey Night in Canada* telecast last season, a grim reminder of how the Oilers shattered the Flames' lofty expectations for the 1987-88 campaign, and raised the doubts about any Calgary title aspirations.

The Flames' coaches set three targets in 1988-89 – 1) play a disciplined, defensive style aimed at allowing the fewest number of goals in the league; 2) win the Presidents' Trophy with most points during the regular season; and 3) win the Stanley Cup. Without the Stanley Cup, the other two achievements would be meaningless.

Rather than bolt out of the starting gate, the Flames started in an inauspicious manner. Their season opener, on October 6 at the Saddledome, watched the rebuilding Islanders (who would finish the year with the second worst record in the NHL) stun the Flames and their fans by assuming a 4–1 lead early in the third period before the Flames stormed back to salvage an unimpressive 4–4 tie.

The Flames' express became derailed in the second game of the season two days later – Calgary's first regular-season look at Gretzky's Kings in southern California. That initial visit to L.A. verified that Kings' owner McNall had indeed struck gold in the tough California market with Gretzky mania. Certainly, I had never seen anything like this during my many trips to California. There was much media hype over hockey, despite the fact the Los Angeles Dodgers were well on their way to a World Series championship.

The City of Angels is really a city of superstars, whether in the motion picture industry or sports. The stars come out to see the stars, so when McNall obtained the biggest name in hockey, Gretzky attracted such a following that the Kings established season attendance records and became covered and talked about in the same breath as the city's major league baseball (Dodgers and Angels), National Basketball Association (Lakers and Clippers), and National Football League (Rams and Raiders) teams.

Sylvester Stallone, John Candy, Sajak, and hordes of other stars became regulars at Kings' games. Newspapers provided the most coverage the Kings had ever received. And Gretzky was everywhere, including billboard advertisements alongside the Lakers' Magic Johnson. The new-look Kings, with Gretzky and the stunning black, silver, and white uniforms, created such a following that the Kings' souvenir shop, located some 15 minutes from the Forum, would be hard-pressed to keep up with the demand.

Record sellouts, record sales, record interest, and legitimate Stanley Cup contenders – Los Angeles would grip every move Gretzky would make looking for a championship to go along with the Laker and Dodger titles of 1988. As if they had to rubberstamp their potential, the Kings received a standout performance by goalie Glen Healy and a controversial overtime goal by Dave Taylor to win that early-season game with Calgary, 6–5.

With one point and 10 goals against after two games, the Flames were hardly on course to attain their expectations. The hockey world was gripped with Gretzky-King fever while the Flames' bandwagon endured the broken-ankle syndrome as fans jumped off following the early disappointments. Before long, though, the Flames would get their game together and let it be known they were ready to enter the race for the top spot in the NHL.

Jiri Hrdina, who would finish with 54 points (22 goals) for the season, emerged as a challenger for the Calder Trophy as rookie of the year with 25 points (12 goals) in the first 20-game quarter of the season. Before the grinding NHL schedule took its toll on Hrdina, he helped ignite the Flames' fire and emerged as the game's first star after a stellar two-way performance in Calgary's first victory of the season, 5–2 over Detroit on October 10 at the Saddledome.

The Flames vaulted ahead of the Oilers with a 6–1 win over Edmonton at Calgary four days later. Doug Gilmour, with three assists and the Molson Cup first-star award, along with another ex-Blue, Mark Hunter, who kayoed Oiler defenceman Kevin Lowe out of the game with a hit into the boards, made their presence felt in their first taste of the Battle of Alberta. Hunter so infuriated the Oilers that several players took runs at him, including Mark Messier, who eventually earned a game misconduct penalty.

Gretzky's debut on Calgary ice in a Kings' uniform occurred on October 17. Amid the unbelievable fanfare, the Flames surged to within one point of the Kings and into fifth place overall by blasting L.A., 11–4. Hrdina, once more, provided early-season offensive power with his first-ever NHL hat trick. The Flames equalled a club record with seven goals in the third period and the 11-goal output was their high for the season. Former Flame assistant coach Pierre Page then brought his North Stars to the Saddledome on October 19 but Calgary's 2–1 win, sparked by a goal and an assist by Gilmour, put Crisp's troops into first place in the Smythe Division and into third overall.

Just when things seemed to be unfolding as predicted one of several trade rumours that emerged during the season appeared, this time in the *Globe and Mail*. During the Flames' first extended road trip, a three-game eastern swing to Toronto, Philadelphia, and Pittsburgh, the report suggested a deal between Calgary and the New York Rangers in which Mike Vernon, Joel Otto, and perhaps Joey Mullen would head east in exchange for goaltender John Vanbiesbrouck and a couple of other players.

I talked to Cliff Fletcher, who acknowledged talks with his Ranger counterpart Phil Esposito during the summer but denied the goaltenders were ever involved in the discussions. Vernon, in the aftermath of the Oiler playoff series, was haunted time and again as being on the trading block, supposedly because of "not being able to win the big one." Fletcher's view was that Vernon and Vanbiesbrouck were among the top six or seven goalies in the NHL and exchanging them would make little difference. When the Flames returned to Calgary after tying (3–3) in Toronto, winning (5–4 in overtime) at Philadelphia, and losing (6–1) at Pittsburgh, Vernon was called into the team's front office and assured he would not be traded. He was told to play to the best of his ability and ignore all rumours.

The Maple Leafs, who would miss the playoffs, were the only team to go undefeated (1–0–2) against Calgary last season. Ken Wregget's 32-save performance gained them the tie on October 22 but the next night the Flames extended their unbeaten streak to six games (5–0–1) when Jim Peplinski's goal at 4:23 of overtime sank the Flyers.

Penguin goaltender Steve Guenette blocked 43 of 44 shots to snap Calgary's unbeaten streak. Guenette made such an impression that the Flames obtained him from Pittsburgh in exchange for a sixth-round 1989 draft choice on January 9, 1989. His addition allowed Calgary to add depth at goaltending as he spent the remainder of the year on the farm at Salt Lake City.

The Flames' 2–2 tie against the Washington Capitals at home three days later made them 5–2–3 – one point better than Los Angeles and fourth overall. Calgary hit its longest tailspin of the season when a 2–1 loss at Vancouver saw them go winless in three.

A 6–3 Halloween night home win over the Chicago Blackhawks propelled the Flames into an 18-game stretch in which they would win 16, tie one, and lose one. They went through November with 10 wins, a loss and a tie. It was around this time that I had my first inkling that this Flame team had that special ingredient to win the Stanley Cup. You could feel something happening and, on the ice where it counted most, the Flames were running up the wins.

The line of Gilmour, Joey Mullen, and Colin Patterson was formed at this time and would remain intact all season. Gilmour, with a goal and three assists, and Mullen, a goal and an assist, spearheaded the 6–1 Flames' home-ice win on November 3 in the first St. Louis-Calgary showdown since the Gilmour trade.

Gilmour's goal and five assists, Mullen's first-ever hat trick as a Flame, and Rick Wamsley's perfect netminding powered Calgary to a 9–0 drubbing of Buffalo two nights later. However, a shoulder separation to Mark Hunter, which would keep him out of eight games, dampened that victory. The Flames completed the three-game home stand when Hrdina tied the club record with four goals en route to a 6–3 harpooning of the Hartford Whalers.

A six-game trek to the East began on November 9 with a downer in Buffalo as hot goaltending by Darren Puppa and two goals by Pierre Turgeon avenged the Sabres' defeat in Calgary the previous week. Buffalo emerged with a 3–2 win despite getting only 12 shots on Wamsley.

The Flames then took off on club records for the longest unbeaten streak (13 games, 12 wins, one loss) and longest road winning streak (seven games) with another overtime win in Philadelphia, 3–2, the next night. This time, Joe Nieuwendyk supplied the overtime winner as the Flames climbed into first place in the overall standings for the first time, two points ahead of Boston and three points up on Los Angeles and Edmonton.

That set the stage for the first-place showdown at Boston Garden on November 12. Vernon received indication from Crisp at that time that he would be the number-one goalie because, for the first time since the sixth game, the coach went with a goalie in two consecutive games. In blocking 36 shots, Vernon outduelled ex-Flame Reggie Lemelin as Hrdina's second-period goal won it, 2–1.

Tim Hunter scored the winner – the last of three goals he produced during the season – and Wamsley turned aside 22 shots in the Flames' 5–1 decision against the Islanders on November 15. The Flames then reached the quarter mark of the season in impressive fashion with a 5–3 verdict over the New Jersey Devils at the Meadowlands on November 17. Hrdina completed his dynamic start to the season with a goal and two assists as the Flames led the pack with 13 victories, four losses, and three ties for 29 points in 20 games. Gilmour, with 27 points, paced Flame scorers through this segment, followed by Hrdina, 25, Mullen, 24, Hakan Loob and Gary Suter, 21 each.

The Kings and the Oilers each trailed the Flames by five points while the Montreal Canadiens, under new coach Pat Burns, felt the pressure early when they were 4–7–1 after 12 games but showed signs of life at 9–8–3 at the first-quarter mark. Those persistent rumours about the possible firing of Burns were, to paraphrase Mark Twain, greatly exaggerated.

The race between Calgary and Montreal for first place overall, for the fewest goals against, and for the Stanley Cup was under way ... and getting hotter.

Brad McCrimmon . . . taking charge. *(Brad Watson photo)*

All tied up . . . Al MacInnis nulli-
fies Quebec's Mike Hough. *(Brad
Watson photo)*

Top: Eye on the man . . . Gary Suter keeps a close watch on this Oiler attacker. *(Brad Watson photo)*

Bottom: Wammer saves . . . Goalie Rick Wamsley kicks out this shot during regular season action against Chicago. *(Brad Watson photo)*

Determination . . . Rob Ramage
and the Islanders' Brent Sutter
duel for the edge. *(Brad Watson
photo)*

Top Left: Assistant Coach Doug Risebrough. *(Brad Watson photo)*

Bottom Left: Assistant coach Tom Watt with head coach Terry Crisp in the background. *(Brad Watson photo)*

Right: Howdy, Sergei . . . The Flames welcomed Sergei Priakin, former captain of the Soviet Wings, in typical Calgary style – the white hat. *(Calgary Sun photo)*

High five for Nieuwy . . . Joe Nieuwendyk proudly displays the pucks that set the club record for most goals by one player in one game. His five-goal explosion came at the Saddledome on January 11, 1989, and triggered an 8–3 romp over the Winnipeg Jets. *(Calgary Sun photo)*

The Canadiens Go Full Thrust

Joey Mullen and Jamie Macoun were fascinating studies throughout the Calgary Flames' season. Mullen, who would capture his second Lady Byng Trophy (as the NHL's most gentlemanly player) in three years, finished seventh in the scoring race with 110 points. Those ahead of him were the Penguins' Mario Lemieux (199), the Kings' Wayne Gretzky (168), the Red Wings' Steve Yzerman (155), the Kings' Bernie Nicholls (150), and the Penguins' Rob Brown (115) and Paul Coffey (113) … select company to be sure, and Mullen deserved to be among them. The 32-year-old Mullen's outstanding season, which included standout performances in the NHL All-Star game and the Stanley Cup playoffs, also resulted in his selection to the NHL First All-Star team, only the second Flame to achieve such standing.

From the start of the 1988-89 season, Joey showed remarkable stamina and set a steady pace for getting points throughout the season – 24 in the first quarter, 29 in the second, 25 in the third, and 32 in the fourth. With the Stanley Cup on the line, he accumulated 24 points in 21 playoff games. During last year's training camp he mentioned that, for the first time in his career, he participated in an off-season training program at his summer home on Cape Cod. Normally a slow starter, Mullen found that the daily running along the Cape Cod beaches and the weight-lifting reaped enormous benefits from start to finish.

Macoun's off-season preparations dated back to 1987 when he dedicated himself to bouncing back from the severe nerve damage to his left arm following the car accident that almost claimed his life. Although he missed the entire 1987-88 term, he promised to return in 1988-89 and contribute to a Flames' championship.

Team behind the team . . . The Flames' wives and girlfriends signify they're No. 1 at the post-Stanley Cup party. *(Brad Watson photo)*

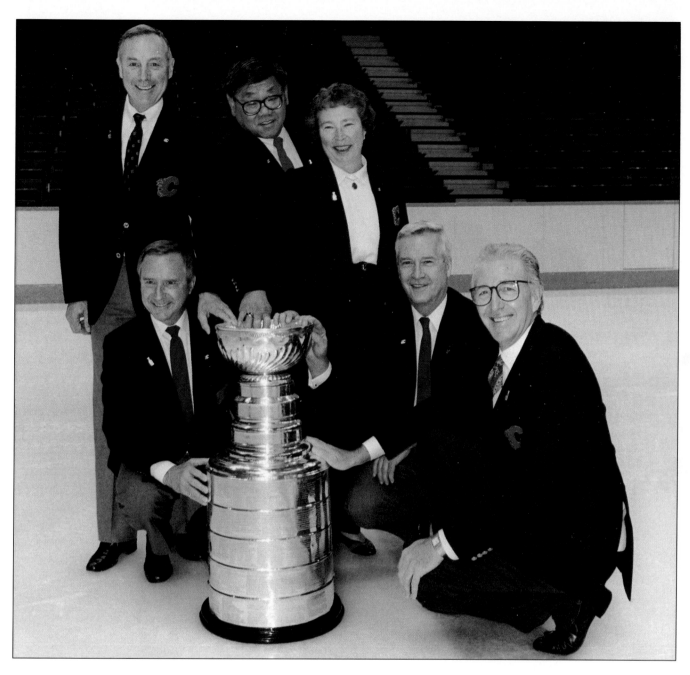

Winning smiles . . . The Calgary
Flames' owners surround the
coveted Stanley Cup. Bottom,
left to right, Byron J. Seaman,
Harley Hotchkiss, Norman Green.
Top, left to right, Daryl (Doc)
Seaman, Norman Kwong, Sonia
Scurfield. *(Brad Watson photo)*

Lining up . . . The unit of (left to right) Hakan Loob, Joe Nieuwendyk, and Gary Roberts scored many big goals through the season. *(Brad Watson photo)*

While he downplayed the physical hurdles and mental anguish on that road back, it was a touching story when he did return.

"Everybody said I did a lot of work, did this and did that, making a grandiose thing out of it," Macoun said. "Anyone in my position would have done the same amount of work. Hey, all I wanted to do was get back."

Macoun played in 72 regular-season games (missing eight games due to a concussion in late January) and all 22 playoff games. Aside from the early stages of the season, when Jamie adjusted to game conditions, he patrolled the blueline with the robust style and speed that are his trademarks.

Mullen, Macoun, and the Flames completed the six-game road trip and began the second quarter of the season with a 5–2 win in Hartford on November 19. Nieuwendyk guided the way with two goals as the Flames, for the first time in club history, won five games on a single road trip.

Lanny McDonald, who played in only nine games in the first quarter, would see action in 45 games the rest of the way, including 13 in the second quarter. He entered the 1988-89 schedule with 489 goals and 499 assists and ambitions to collect his 500th goal, 500th assist, 1,000th point, and the Stanley Cup. The Flames opened a four-game home stand on November 23 with a 3–2 victory over the Devils and McDonald snapped the winning goal (his first tally of the season) at 11:15 of the third period.

Instead of alternating goalies, Crisp once more went back-to-back with Mike Vernon when he started against the Kings three days later. The Kings trailed Calgary by three points entering the game and grabbed a 1–0 lead. But two goals and an assist by Mullen and Vernon's 28-save brilliance, which earned him number-one star, cemented Calgary's seventh consecutive win, 4–1.

The pesky Canucks almost defeated the Flames again but were unable to maintain their two-goal lead and settled for a 3–3 tie at the Saddledome on November 29. Doug Gilmour's power-play goal in the third period evened the score for Calgary.

Guy Lafleur made his Calgary debut as a New York Ranger on December 1 and the cheers he drew when hitting the goalpost indicated The Flower still has quite a southern Alberta following. The night belonged to the Flames, though, as Colin Patterson, back after missing two games because of a concussion, scored 43 seconds into the game, Nieuwendyk supplied his second consecutive two-goal game (third of the season), and McDonald moved into 14th place on the all-time scoring list with his 491st goal. Calgary triumphed 6–3 to begin what became a five-game winning streak.

The Battle of Alberta II swung into Edmonton on December 2 with feelings still heated over the first meeting in Calgary in mid-October. McDonald's 492nd career goal sparked the Flames' 7–4 triumph as Calgary opened a six-point cushion for first overall over Los Angeles and Montreal.

McDonald achieved his 500th career assist milestone on December 4, assisting on the final goal (by Jim Peplinski), and Gary Roberts scored twice during a 6–3 setback of the Jets in Winnipeg for Calgary's record-setting seventh straight road win.

At this stage of the season, the unit of Nieuwendyk between his childhood friend Roberts and Hakan Loob was formed and remained together for the rest of the season. Back-to-back home wins on December 6 (3–2 over Quebec) and on December 8 (5–3 over Edmonton) established the Flames' record to 13 games without a loss (12–0–1). In only their 28th game of the season, the Flames became the first NHL team to register 20 wins (against the Nordiques) as Al MacInnis broke the tie late in the third period.

Nieuwendyk became the first Flame to hit the 20-goal mark in the season when he connected against the Oilers, Calgary's 29th contest. Gilmour notched the first goal against Edmonton and extended his scoring streak to 11 games (four goals, 11 assists). This signified the longest regular-season scoring streak of any Flame in 1988-89 but fell five games short of Gary Suter's team record, set at the end of the 1987-88 season.

The Whalers extinguished the Flames' unbeaten streak and seven-game road winning streak, along with the five-game winning streak, with a neat, disciplined 4–1 count at Hartford on December 10.

Two days later, the Flames were once more held to a tie by the Maple Leafs as a slumping Al Secord, with only one goal entering the game (against Calgary in their first meeting), supplied two more in the 4–4 stalemate. Jeff Reese outguessed Nieuwendyk on a first-period penalty shot but he was unable to prevent Mullen from becoming the second Flame to reach the 20-goal mark. Peplinski, who honed his skills as a Marlboro at Maple Leaf Gardens, earned his 400th career point and Loob his 200th NHL assist.

The Flames went home-and-home with the Canucks on December 15-16. Rick Wamsley blocked 28 shots in the 2–0 victory at the Saddledome, then the next night Nieuwendyk converted a penalty shot in the second period on Steve Weeks to trigger the 5–3 win at the Pacific Coliseum. The sweep planted the Flames seven points ahead of Montreal in the overall standings and made them the first over 50 points in the season (23–5–5 for 51 points).

With three full days between games, the Flames flew directly from Vancouver to Los Angeles for a bit of a respite before the

December 20 game against the Kings. However, the Kings were sharp and, led by the fifth hat trick in his career, former Flame John Tonelli sparked Los Angeles to the 7–3 decision. Mullen came down with the flu and would sit out his only game of the regular season on December 23 at Edmonton.

Normally, the Flames would return on the direct flight from Los Angeles to Calgary on the afternoon of the next day. But in order to get home for the team's family Christmas party, the Flames departed earlier, via Salt Lake City. This flight became probably the roughest of the year for the Flames as the airplane ran into heavy turbulence before settling in for the bumpy flight to Salt Lake City. Once the plane landed in Salt Lake City, Roberts and Nieuwendyk went to assistant to the president Al Coates and asked how much it would cost to rent a car for a drive back to Calgary. As the call was made to board the plane for the connection to Calgary, Peplinski quipped: "Let's saddle up, boys, and head on to Calgary." That flight was much smoother and the party went on, although delayed until the players arrived.

The Oilers were hardly in the gift-giving mood in the pre-Christmas tilt at Northlands Coliseum. For the first and only time during the regular season, the Flames lost two consecutive games. A penalty-shot goal by Craig MacTavish and the goaltending of Grant Fuhr led the Oilers to a 4–1 win.

That loss, combined with a Montreal win in Boston the previous night, dropped Calgary one point behind the Canadiens in the overall standings (52 points for Montreal, 51 for Calgary) and only three in front of the Kings. The Flames, however, went into the Christmas break with four games in hand on Montreal and three on the Kings.

Nieuwendyk's overtime goal, with the Canucks two men short, provided a 3–2 Boxing Day win in Vancouver and vaulted Calgary into temporary possession of first overall on the idle Canadiens. On Tuesday, December 27, the Flames returned to the Saddledome for an exhibition match against Riga Dynamo of the Soviet Union. While the Flames scored a 4–2 victory, their attention was focused at the Great Western Forum where the Canadiens doubled the Kings 4–2 to regain first by a point.

The interest reached Stanley Cup proportions on December 29 when the Canadiens and the Flames staged their first showdown of the season. After a scoreless first period, the Canadiens erupted for four goals in the second period, including three goals in less than three minutes and two within 34 seconds. Mats Naslund counted two goals in the Canadiens' 4–3 triumph. The Flames almost came back with a strong performance in the latter part of the game, but round one went to the Canadiens, who now stood at 25–10–6 for 56 points after 41 games. The Flames, in absorbing their first loss at home in the 1988-89 season after a string of 17 games without a loss (14–0–3), still had three games to go before their halfway point.

The letdown after the loss to the Canadiens was evident on New Year's Eve as the Flames let a 4–0 lead escape and settled for a 4–4 draw against the visiting Winnipeg Jets. It was immediately after this game that the Flames promoted Theoren Fleury from Salt Lake City. His NHL debut, against the Nordiques at the Saddledome, put him against the man he tied for the Western Hockey League scoring title in 1987-88, Joe Sakic. Fleury made an instant impact with the crowd and, while he was held pointless, the Flames showed spark with their 5–1 triumph over Quebec.

The Flames rounded out their first half on January 5 with an 8–6 shootout win at home over the Kings. Mullen equalled the Flames' record with four goals and Fleury earned three assists on the night. Doug Gilmour notched his 400th career point and Joel Otto his 200th in that victory as the Flames moved to within two points of the Canadiens and nine points up on the Kings.

The Flames were models of consistency over the first two quarters, winning 13, losing four, and tying three each time. Their 40-game total (26–8–6 for 58 points) had been the best in the NHL – Montreal's total over the same period had been 24–10–6 for 54 points. But the Canadiens were charging, and fast, with their 15–2–3 record and an .825 clip in the second quarter of the season.

The Canadiens and the Flames were in a race to the wire … and then some.

Sizzling Series of Events

The Presidents' Trophy, presented to the NHL by its Board of Governors in 1985-86, is awarded to the club with the best regular-season record. The winning team receives $200,000 to be split between the team and its players. The Stanley Cup winners in 1989 would share in a $525,000 playoff bonus. The pursuit of the Presidents' Trophy and the quest for the Stanley Cup are separate, but they are similar in that the team maintaining high-quality consistency participates in the glory, honour, and monetary rewards.

The Montreal Canadiens' torrid third-quarter tempo translated into tough times if the Flames were not able to match or surpass the oncharging bleu-blanc-rouge express. Montreal compiled a scorching 15–5–0 mark (30 points) through the 20 games in its third quarter; Calgary's Flames fanned an even hotter hand with 15 wins, three losses, and two ties for 32 points!

The Flames accomplished this even though their third quarter began in Jekyll/Hyde fashion. In their back-to-back series on successive nights against the Oilers, the Flames looked like world-beaters in Calgary, winning 7–2, and Stanley Cup pretenders in Edmonton, losing 6–0. Doug Gilmour chipped in with two goals while Theoren Fleury scored his first NHL marker in support of Rick Wamsley's 36-save backstopping of the victory at home. Mark Messier's two goals and Bill Ranford's first NHL shutout handed the Flames their worst beating of the 1988-89 season – and only one of two times they were held goalless.

Joe Nieuwendyk shot into prominence on January 11 at home against the Winnipeg Jets as he set the Flames' single-game scoring record with five goals in an 8–3 rout of the Winnipeg Jets. He equalled the NHL record with four goals in the second period and came within one goal of equalling the modern-day single-game scoring record, last accomplished by the Maple Leafs' Darryl Sittler against Boston on February 6, 1976.

On the night of his banner performance, which included an NHL record 10 points, Sittler remarked: "It was one of those nights when everything happened. Some nights you have the puck and nothing happens. It'll be hard to forget something like this." Lanny McDonald, a close friend of Sittler's, was Darryl's right winger that night and contributed a goal and three assists to the 11–4 win over Don Cherry's Bruins. McDonald did not play on Nieuwendyk's five-goal night but he notified Joe during the second intermission that he had a chance not only to tie the modern-day record last equalled by Sittler – but to surpass it. Lanny then told Joe to go for it!

Only a sharp glove save by Winnipeg goalie Daniel Berthiaume early in the third period prevented a sixth goal by Nieuwendyk. Still, it was quite a memorable night for Joe, who, almost word-for-word in the manner Sittler described that occasion 13 years before in Toronto, said: "It seemed like everything I touched went into the net." Not quite, of course, since he had eight shots on goal, but five out of eight is a remarkable accomplishment nonetheless. He scored once in the first period and four of five Calgary goals in the second. His performance consisted of three power-play tallies, one even-strength marker, and one short-handed goal – scored in a variety of ways, from a couple of tip-ins to having Winnipeg players draped over him, to being knocked down.

Nieuwendyk's showing offset a game in which 252 minutes in penalties were assessed. During the team flight to Minnesota following that game, Joe asked me to show him my *NHL Official Guide & Record Book* and he was fascinated by the names of those who'd scored six goals in a game, and that Joe Malone scored seven goals for the Quebec Bulldogs in 1920 – to think he was flirting with standards set by such elite company!

The Flames still couldn't get on a roll through the first two games of a pivotal six-game road trip, tying Minnesota, 1–1, and losing to the injury-riddled Sabres, 3–2. Those games proved costly: Gary Roberts was shelved for four games with a bad back and Lanny McDonald broke his nose in Buffalo; and trainer Jim (Bearcat) Murray, the only trainer I know of who has a fan club, formed in Boston and now with chapters in Toronto and Montreal, sustained an eye injury in Minnesota. As he administered to a Flame player at the bench, the puck struck him near the right eye. He was sidelined for the trip, but fortunately the injury was not serious. Bearcat, noted for his quickness in running onto the ice to assist injured players, would later gain notoriety during an incident in the Los Angeles series.

The Flames put together impressive 7–1 and 7–2 wins in Detroit and Boston, respectively, and it appeared they were about to unfold another long winning streak. The game in Detroit had been billed as a preview of the Campbell Conference final, but the Flames dominated the Red Wings as Joey Mullen scored twice to become the second Flame at 30 goals (Nieuwendyk had done so six days earlier against Winnipeg). Mullen's linemates, Colin Patterson and Doug Gilmour, each added a goal and two assists while McDonald picked up career point 995 on Dana Murzyn's first goal of the season.

Two nights later on January 19 at Boston Garden, Mark Hunter broke out of a 17-game goalless slump in a grand manner with four goals against the Bruins. Those goals, Hunter's first since December 6, raised his total to 11 and snapped what had been a frustrating stretch for him.

The Flames were then stunned, 4–3, by the Nordiques at Le Colisée in Quebec City on Saturday, January 21, a loss that left them five points behind Montreal heading into their second game against the Canadiens two days later at the Forum. Montreal, having played 51 games, carried a 33–12–6 record; the Flames, after 48 games, stood at 30–11–7 and could ill afford a second defeat to the Canadiens.

This showdown became the best game I saw during the 1988-89 regular season as two great teams turned in a standout display of hockey in a 3–1 Calgary win. Mullen's second-period goal proved to be the winner and Nieuwendyk clinched it with his second goal of the game, and 35th of the year, on a power play late in the third period. It was a particularly satisfying game for Nieuwendyk, who felt the Canadiens had taken several liberties with him during a game in Montreal the previous season.

The same couldn't be said for Jamie Macoun. The thrill of the key victory was offset by a Stephane Richer shot that caught Macoun on the head, resulting in a concussion that kept him out of the next seven games. His helmet prevented more serious injury, but if Al MacInnis possesses the hardest shot in the NHL, Richer isn't far behind – and Macoun can attest to that.

The conquest of the Canadiens ignited the Flames to their second longest unbeaten streak of the season as they went 11–0–1 in that 12-game stretch, one game short of the club record they'd established earlier in the season.

The Flames returned home with a 5–3 win over the New York Rangers on January 26 as Mike Vernon registered his 100th career victory. The Chicago Blackhawks were at the Saddledome less than 48 hours later and, after falling behind 3–0, the Flames fought back to win, 5–4, on Murzyn's overtime goal. Gilmour figured prominently in the comeback with two goals.

The next night, Nieuwendyk's clutch goal late in the second period and Roberts's career-high 15th goal were factors in the Flames' hard-fought 4–4 tie at Vancouver. The point earned lifted Calgary to 74 on the season (from 52 games) and put them even with Montreal in points, although the Canadiens had played two more games.

The Joes, Nieuwendyk and Mullen, each scored hat tricks on January 31, pacing the Flames to an 8–5 decision over the hometown Los Angeles Kings. Nieuwendyk thus climbed to 40 goals and Mullen to 35 as the Flames began what would become their longest winning streak of the season, eight games. The win padded Calgary's lead over Los Angeles to 18 points.

Nieuwendyk's sharpshooting netted his second overtime goal of the season as Calgary returned home to defeat Detroit, 3–2, on February 2. Then, for the first time in regular-season action, the Flames hosted the Canucks on consecutive days, February 4 and 5. The doubleheader, won 5–2 and 5–4 by the Flames, put Calgary at 37–11–8 heading into the three-day NHL All-Star break. Mullen's two goals triggered the first triumph over Vancouver while Hakan Loob scored the winner and added two assists in the second clash. The Presidents' Trophy challenge with the pause in the schedule positioned Montreal with 57 games played and a record of 37–14–6 for 80 points and Calgary, with 82 points from 56 games, stood at 37–11–8.

All attention in the hockey world turned to Edmonton for the 40th NHL All-Star game and associated festivities. The return of Wayne Gretzky to lead the Clarence Campbell Conference team against the Prince of Wales Conference dominated news from this event. Edmontonians eagerly awaited the reunion of Gretzky with Jari Kurri and they certainly did not disappoint as the two hit for early goals.

The Flames, for the second consecutive year, were represented by a club record four players – Mike Vernon, Gary Suter, Joey Mullen, and Joe Nieuwendyk, the latter a late replacement for injured Chicago centre Denis Savard. There was some doubt Nieuwendyk would participate since an ankle injury kept him out of the Flames' previous game against Vancouver, but he had recovered sufficiently to suit up for the game. All the Flame players played well in helping the Campbell Conference to a 9–5 win, snapping the Wales' four-game winning streak. Mullen scored two goals to continue his exceptional season and many felt he could have been selected the game MVP, but that honour went to the man of the hour, Gretzky.

NHL regular-season action resumed on February 9 with the Flames playing in St. Louis, the first game for Gilmour and Hunter at the St. Louis Arena since the trade the previous September. Gilmour was the centre of much media attention but he handled the pressure well, going from early morning radio shows to late post-game interviews. He capped a glorious return to St. Louis with two goals and an assist to propel the Flames to a 5–3 win. The crowd provided several loud ovations, saving the best for when he was introduced as the game's number-one star.

The ensuing weekend stops in Washington and Pittsburgh plus a February 15 game at Winnipeg produced three more victories: 2–1 (over the Capitals), 4–2 (over the Penguins), and 6–1 (over the Jets). Nieuwendyk's second-period power-play goal was the difference in Washington. Against Pittsburgh, the Flames peppered Penguin goalie Wendell Young with 50 shots and got two goals from Gilmour. The win over Pittsburgh gave Calgary its 40th win in the team's 59th game – the fastest the Flames had ever won 40 games in a season. It also terminated Pittsburgh's six-game overall and four-game home winning streaks over the Flames.

The Flames reached the three-quarter mark of the season at Winnipeg by extending their NHL-leading record to 41–11–8 for 90 points, good enough for an eight-point lead over Montreal for first overall and 25 in front of Los Angeles for first place in the Smythe Division. The Winnipeg game marked the first time Theoren Fleury's father saw him play an NHL game in person and the youngster responded with a goal and an assist. Loob scored his 20th goal of the season. The balanced attack of the Flames is highlighted by the team's leading scorers in the third quarter of the season. For those 20 games, Mullen and Gilmour each generated 25 points, Joe with 13 goals and Doug with 10. Loob had 24 points, while Nieuwendyk supplied 23 points in the 19 games he played – 19 of them goals. A couple of blueliners, Suter and MacInnis, each garnered 20 points in the third quarter.

The Flames' solid drive had opened up some breathing room between themselves and the Canadiens, but Montreal would win its 60th game and move to within six points in the overall standings. The stretch drive would not permit any letup.

A grand cake . . . Lanny
McDonald prepares to blow out
the candles on the cake in honour of his 1,000th career point.
(Brad Watson photo)

500 big ones . . . Jim Peplinski (right) presents Lanny McDonald with the puck from his milestone 500th goal. *(Brad Watson photo)*

Inset: Lanny's 500th! . . . Lanny McDonald used his patented wrap-around play to become a member of the select 500-goal club, beating the Islanders' Mark Fitzpatrick at the Saddledome on March 21. *(Calgary Sun photo)*

Above: 1,000th point a goal . . . He hoped he'd score a goal for his 1,000th career point and that's exactly what Lanny McDonald did against Winnipeg's Bob Essensa on March 7. *(Calgary Sun photo)*

Right Down to the Wire

The home stretch for the Calgary Flames began with enough unanswered questions to create intense drama. Among them:

- Would the Flames hold off the Montreal Canadiens? With 20 games to go, Calgary was ahead by six points.
- Would Joe Nieuwendyk match his 51-goal production from his rookie award-winning season? He entered the last quarter with 43 goals.
- Would Joe Mullen crack the 50-goal and 100-point circles? Through the first three quarters, he stood at 39 goals and 78 points.
- Would Lanny McDonald reach 500 goals and 1,000 points? He had scored four goals and seven assists through the 35 games he dressed for to bring his career totals to 493 goals and 999 points.

The chapter written in the final 20 games of the regular season should have served as an omen that 1988-89 belonged to the Flames. Despite what loomed as enormous challenges and, in some cases, seemingly insurmountable tasks, those questions would each be answered by a resounding *yes*.

Injuries, as they always are, became an unexpected obstacle that placed greater burdens on those fit enough to play. The Flames, who recorded 92 man-games lost throughout the entire 1988-89 campaign, suffered 47 of those in the final quarter.

The defence was hardest hit, when Gary Suter missed 16 games beginning on February 22 with an appendectomy and then Dana Murzyn (strained knee) and Brad McCrimmon (bruised foot) were sidelined for seven games each starting on March 14. Doug Gilmour's abscessed jaw resulted in a six-game absence from

March 7 to March 21. While these players returned in late March, it would require some playing time in the first round of the play-offs before they regained their top level. In the case of Suter, even worse was to befall him during the playoffs.

The final quarter of the season kicked off on February 18 when the Boston Bruins overcame a two-goal deficit and defeated the Flames, 4–3, at the Saddledome. In the process, the Bruins became only the second team to win on Calgary ice to that point and it's noteworthy that of the Flames' four regular-season losses on home ice, three were at the hands of Adams Division teams (Montreal twice and Boston). The Bruins' triumph stopped the Calgary winning streak at eight games and also curtailed the 12-game (11–0–1) unbeaten streak.

The Flames found the winning form two nights later when, led by Hakan Loob's goal and two assists, they jumped to a 6–0 lead en route to a 6–2 home-ice triumph over the Washington Capitals. The win did have a price, though, as Joel Otto suffered a thumb injury that put him out of the lineup for four games.

Jeff Reese backstopped the visiting Toronto Maple Leafs to a 4–3 overtime win over the Flames on February 22. In an earlier game against Calgary, Reese stopped Nieuwendyk on a penalty shot; this time he outguessed Loob. The Flames came back from a three-goal deficit before Gary Leeman settled the issue, giving the lowly Leafs a win and two ties in three games against Calgary. Mullen reached the 40-goal mark for the sixth consecutive season in that loss to Toronto.

On February 24, Jamie Macoun's winning goal, after Calgary squandered a three-goal lead, gave the Flames a 4–3 victory over the St. Louis Blues. Gary Roberts reached a milestone in that game with his first 20-goal season. Two nights later, rookie goalie Bob Essensa, a newcomer to the Jets' lineup, kicked aside 24 shots in Winnipeg as the Flames went home empty, 1–0.

The next night at the Saddledome Calgary beat Philadelphia, 6–2, and welcomed back Rob Ramage from his eight-game sus-pension for a high-sticking incident at Buffalo in January. Mullen showed the way to victory over the Flyers with a goal and two assists while Perry Berezan scored the Flames' final goal – and his last in a Calgary uniform. Berezan, popular among his teammates and the Calgary community, endured an injury-riddled 1987-88 season but was unable to crack the Flames' lineup last term. On Friday, March 3, the day after the Flames were defeated 3–2 by the Montreal Canadiens in another terrific meeting of these giants, Berezan was traded to Minnesota for Brian MacLellan, a big left winger who Calgary management believed would loom large in the Stanley Cup chase.

Berezan, an Edmontonian, is credited with one of the most significant goals in Flames' history – the goal the Oilers' Steve Smith inadvertently put into his own net in the seventh game of the 1986 Smythe Division final. The Flames captured that game as a result, 3–2, and eliminated the two-time champion Oilers.

Brent Gilchrist figured notably in Montreal's second win in two meetings with the Flames at Calgary by scoring the winning goal midway through the third period and by administering the check to Gilmour that precipitated the abscessed jaw. Joel Otto, as he generally does in big games, made his offensive presence felt by counting both Flame goals.

The Canadiens not only captured the season series with Calgary, two games to one, but also moved to within one point of the Flames for the Presidents' Trophy. Each club had 13 games to play. Calgary, to this point, had a 44–15–8 record for 96 points; Montreal stood at 44–16–7 for 95 points.

For head coach Terry Crisp, a valuable lesson was learned after he lost his cool during a penalty call to the Flames, which resulted in a goal by Montreal's Petr Svoboda. Crisp told me he may have blown the game by overreacting and getting his players' minds off the job at hand in an important game. This experience would later pay off.

Lanny McDonald caught fire over a seven-game stretch beginning March 7 against Winnipeg and ending March 21 against the Islanders. The Jets' Essensa could not bar the door this time as McDonald's 494th goal and 1,000th career point at 2:46 of the first period touched off early fireworks in Calgary's 9–5 decision at the Saddledome. Mark Hunter paced the attack with three goals but the night belonged to Lanny. It was a typical McDonald wraparound goal, a trademark he would re-create down the line for another special moment.

"I think it (the 1,000th point) meant a heck of a lot more because it was a goal," McDonald said. "I didn't think I could get as excited as I did about the 1,000 points and maybe that had something to do with waiting four or five games to get it. But I really was glad it was a goal and especially the way it was scored, it seemed like kind of my own play and I couldn't have been happier."

The Flames' Joel Otto limited Pittsburgh's Mario Lemieux to one shot on goal as Calgary thumped the Penguins, 10–3, on March 9. Otto also provided his 20th goal but Nieuwendyk proved to be top gun with two goals and three assists while Loob and McDonald also hit for two goals apiece. The win was Mike Vernon's 30th, marking the third consecutive year he eclipsed the 30-win mark.

McDonald carried his hot hand into Edmonton at the start of a four-game road trip as his 497th and 498th career goals ignited a Calgary comeback in a 5–5 tie with the Oilers that provided the Flames a second straight 100-point season. The two multiple-goal games heightened the excitement in the countdown to 500. The Flames' trip to New York City on March 13 generated even more hype in that Lanny's idol, Gordie Howe, scored his 500th goal against the Rangers' Gump Worsley on March 14, 1962, at Madison Square Garden.

The 1988-89 Rangers, with Phil Esposito as general manager and Guy Lafleur and Marcel Dionne in the lineup, had three 500-goal men present when McDonald and the Flames came to town. Unfortunately, Lanny failed to score and the Rangers upset the Flames, 4–3, as Calgary fell two points behind Montreal with nine games to play.

MacLellan's first goal as a Flame and Nieuwendyk's 49th of the season shot Calgary to a 5–1 win over the New Jersey Devils the following night at the Meadowlands. Following this game, the Flames went to Newport Beach, California, for three days of rest and relaxation before making the hour's drive to Inglewood for the March 18 contest with the Kings. Flames' management believed, with the grind of the regular schedule and the upcoming playoffs, the side trip away from hockey would be time well spent.

The Flames stormed to the attack when they got back to hockey business by blasting the Kings, 9–3, at the sold-out Great Western Forum. Mark Hunter generated another three-goal game and McDonald moved yet closer to No. 500 with his 499th.

I recall when Lanny pursued his 300th and 400th goals he required a few games to connect. But he wasted absolutely no time for No. 500 as it came in the very next game, on March 21 against the New York Islanders at the Saddledome. On the same night, Nieuwendyk followed McDonald's milestone with one of his own – his 50th goal for the second consecutive season. He thus became one of only three players to score 50 goals in each of his first two seasons (Mike Bossy and Wayne Gretzky were the others).

McDonald scored at 10:54 of the first period and padded the Flames' lead to 2–0 on the way to a 4–1 win. Once more, McDonald's trusty wrap-around accomplished the trick as he came out from behind the net and stuffed the puck past Mark Fitzpatrick to become only the 14th player in NHL history to reach the 500-goal plateau. He immediately leaped into an embrace with Otto and co-captain Jim Peplinski and the crowd erupted into a lengthy standing ovation as referee Bob Myers allowed the occasion to be savoured. Lanny found an instant to give his wife, Ardell, the thumbs-up sign for the special moment.

"The funny part about the 1,000th point and the 500th goal was that both goalies were rookies and Wammer (Rick Wamsley) and Vernie (Vernon) both said since they likely hadn't seen the wrap-around to go for it if I got the chance," McDonald said. "Talk about a dream come true, holy smokes. The seven goals in seven games was a hell of a way to go, especially since a lot of people had written me off a long time before that.

"Ardell and I had always talked about if I could get on a roll, get some momentum, anything was possible. I felt that even if I had four or five games to go and still needed those seven goals that somehow I would get it. It's amazing how driven you become when you're getting close to something like that ... you realize how badly you really want it."

One of the amusing incidents in the aftermath of No. 500 occurred in the McDonald household the next day.

"The newspaper listed the 500-goal scorers and Leah, our nine-year-old, was going through the list and said: 'Dad, Wayne Gretzky's got 635 goals and you've got only 500!' " McDonald said, chuckling. "Then she looks across at Wayne's name and says, 'Aw, Dad, he did it in 10 seasons and you had to do it in 16!' So, it kind of brings you down to earth in a heck of a hurry but it was a lot of fun."

The Presidents' Trophy hunt remained even on March 23 when the Flames defeated the Kings, 4–2, at the Saddledome. Theoren Fleury paced the attack with two goals and Mullen attained his first 100-point season when he assisted on the first of Gilmour's two goals in the game. An altercation between the Kings' Jim Wiemer and Otto resulted in the Flames' centre being suspended three games for abusing linesman Ron Finn. The Flames were minus Otto for a three-game road trip in four nights commencing March 24 in Winnipeg.

Calgary failed to take possession of first place when Randy Carlyle's overtime goal sank them, 4–3, against the Jets. Stunned by that loss, the Flames thought they'd lost their chance for first overall until Minnesota rekindled those hopes by tying Montreal on March 25. The following night, the Flames grabbed first place thanks to a four-goal blitz by Mullen, which helped overcome a 4–2 deficit and defeat the Blackhawks, 7–5, at Chicago Stadium. That was the first time Mullen scored four goals in an NHL game.

"Until this happened, I thought my chances of having a 50-goal season would go down the drain," said Mullen, who broke a three-game famine with his outburst in Chicago.

On the afternoon of that Sunday night game, Mullen and McDonald spent time in church. "After mass ended, the two of us sat and visited in the church for about 10 or 15 minutes," McDonald recalled. "It was one of the nicest visits Mully and I had ever had and we've roomed together for about four years … it was very special. And then he went and scored four goals!"

Mullen wasn't finished either, as he scored his 49th in the next night's 3–2 win at Minnesota. Montreal's triumph over Boston the same night gave the Canadiens 112 points – one fewer than the Flames – with two games left for each team.

The Flames were exactly where they wanted to be – in control of their own destiny. Under the tie-breaking formula, Calgary would get first overall if it finished with the same number of points as the Canadiens. Montreal assumed one final brief grip of first place with its 4–2 victory at Buffalo on March 30, but the Flames followed the next night by taking control again as Joey Mullen's 50th goal sparked a 4–1 home win over Winnipeg.

On April 1, the Canadiens, needing a victory to keep their hopes for first alive, tied Philadelphia, 2–2, at home to earn 115 points on the season. The Presidents' Trophy belonged to the Flames for a second successive season.

Despite a meaningless last home game against Edmonton on April 2 in which Al MacInnis, Loob, Roberts, and Nieuwendyk sat out, the Flames completed the regular season with a 4–2 triumph anyway. Mullen chalked up his 51st goal in that one to tie Nieuwendyk for the club lead at the end of the regular season.

In scoring, the final quarter was Mullen's best with 32 points, 12 of them goals. Fleury added 17 points in the 17 games he played in the final quarter and Ric Nattress saw the most action he'd seen in the year because the injury-plagued blueline resulted in him playing, and being effective, in 19 of the 20 games. Mark Hunter finished in a flurry with 10 goals in the final quarter while Jiri Hrdina made a comeback with 15 points.

The Flames, 13–6–1 in the final quarter, finished with a 54–17–9 record for 117 points. Along the way they established ten team and eight individual records. And they had answered all the questions that faced them heading into the final 20 games. The Flames finished first overall; Nieuwendyk reached 51 goals again, as did Mullen, who captured the team scoring lead with 110 points. And Lanny, well, he became a separate story altogether.

There was only one question left: Would the Calgary Flames win the Stanley Cup?

Squeeze play . . . Defenceman
Jamie Macoun and goalie Mike
Vernon manage to crunch
Chicago's Steve Thomas during
Game 5 of the Campbell final.
(Calgary Sun photo)

Alain holds fort . . . Chicago
goalie Alain Chevrier helped the
Blackhawks to a strong playoff
performance. Here, he blocks the
Flames' Tim Hunter, but it wasn't
enough as the Flames captured
the Campbell Conference final in
five games. *(Calgary Sun photo)*

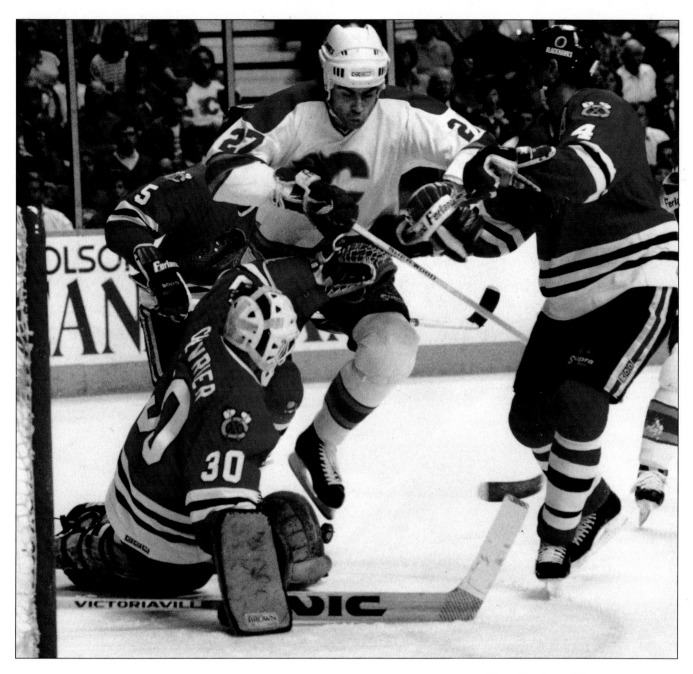

Big Mac attack . . . Brian MacLellan, noted for his toughness, scored the winner during the fifth and deciding game against Chicago. MacLellan, seen causing havoc around Alain Chevrier, and two goals by Joe Nieuwendyk gave Calgary a 3–1 win. *(Calgary Sun photo)*

Great inspiration . . . Joe
Nieuwendyk showed his true grit
in the '89 playoffs, performing
despite injuries that would have
put most others on the sidelines.
This action occurred just a game
after he sustained serious injuries
to the mouth as the Flames eliminated the Blackhawks in the
fifth game of the Campbell final.
(Calgary Sun photo)

It's tough out there . . . Flames' defenceman Ric Nattress knocks the helmet off Chicago's Steve Larmer during the opening game of the Campbell Conference final, a 3–0 Calgary win. *(Calgary Sun photo)*

Rough ride . . . Joey Mullen is
taken into the boards by Chicago
defenceman Dave Manson during the second game of the
Campbell Conference final.
(Calgary Sun photo)

The Big Scare

**he 14th place Vancouver Canucks** weren't given much chance of winning more than a game, let alone upsetting the Calgary Flames in the opening round of the Stanley Cup playoffs. After all, they'd finished 43 points behind the Flames, and their 33–39–8 record for fourth place in the Smythe Division paled miserably to that of the Flames.

But these Canucks were vastly improved from the club that missed the playoffs in 1987-88. The Canucks had registered a 25 per cent increase in points over the previous season; Calgary, by comparison, had raised its point total by a little over 11 per cent.

The Flames had committed themselves to disciplined, defensive hockey in 1988-89, and so had the Canucks. The Flames scored 43 fewer goals in 1988-89 than they had the season before and finished with 354 goals (second to the Kings' 376), but at the same time they reduced their goals against from 305 in 1987-88 to 226 (second to Montreal's 218). Vancouver, for its part, had cut its goals against by 67. The Flames, therefore, were up against the third best defensive team in 1988-89 when they started the playoffs. And when the playoffs begin, the team with the finest defensive game usually wins.

Heavily favoured, the Flames sported a 5–1–2 record against Vancouver during the regular season. The spread in goals, though, indicated much closer competition as Calgary outscored the Canucks, 28–20. Flames' assistant GM Al MacNeil sensed a fear of Vancouver as early as mid-February when he told me: "It bothers me that in the eight games against the Canucks this season we didn't establish our authority because we didn't blow them away in any of the games."

The experts still predicted a Calgary victory in four or five games. Instead, Calgary was fortunate to escape elimination as the Canucks came closest to snuffing that dream of the Eternal Flames. The series came down to overtime in the seventh game at the Saddledome on April 15. A puck centred by Jim Peplinski went off Joel Otto's skate as the Flame centre jammed the front of the net and skipped past Vancouver goalie Kirk McLean for the winning goal at 19:21. Calgary 4, Vancouver 3.

That's how the game was decided on the scoresheet, but the truth is that without Mike Vernon's spectacular play the Flames were, to quote that famous hockey philosopher, Tiger Williams, "done like dinner." The Canucks dominated the third period when Doug Lidster scored the equalizer, then had the edge in the overtime. But Vernon, exerting himself like someone who simply would not be beaten, pulled off three cases of grand larceny in overtime. The point-blank toe save off Petri Skriko and the glove-hand robbery off Tony Tanti and Stan Smyl rescued the flickering Flames until Otto used his massive size to create havoc at the Vancouver net and end the suspense.

"If it hadn't been for Vernie, there'd have been no time for me to get the winning goal," Otto told me. "He just kept saving us. Nobody, but nobody, should be asked the question now whether Mike Vernon can win the big game."

The hard-fought series concluded almost as it began – with a 4–3 overtime game at the Saddledome. However, that first game of the series on April 5 went to the Canucks, thanks to the deciding shot by former Flame defenceman Paul Reinhart. The Flames and their fans were literally stunned by that marker. Rarely have I heard any hockey arena, especially the Saddledome, as quiet. Doug Barkley and I were doing the post-game wrap-up and it felt like our voices could be heard throughout the arena … it was that silent.

The Canucks, playing within their limitations, proved their point. They were not going to wilt, they were not going to listen to their detractors. They were intent on winning.

Now the pressure rested on Calgary. The Flames had lost their home-ice advantage and could ill afford a loss the next night. The tenseness they'd shown in Game 1 disappeared in Game 2 as the Flames, on first-period goals by Otto and Colin Patterson, along with a strong two-way effort by Hakan Loob, tied the series with a 5–2 win.

The Pacific Coliseum welcomed the Canucks home with a wildly enthusiastic crowd for Game 3 but the Flames dampened that spirit with a 4–0 victory despite only 15 shots on McLean. Vernon, with 21 saves, picked up his first-ever playoff shutout, and the first of three to his credit in the 1989 playoffs. Loob played another strong game with a goal while the Flames' leading goal scorers, Joe Mullen and Joe Nieuwendyk, also had a goal apiece.

The coaching profession, it seems, is only as good as one's last win. When Terry Crisp made some lineup changes, resting Mark Hunter and Brian MacLellan while scratching Mullen because of the flu, he was heavily criticized following the 5–3 loss in Game 4. The power plays dominated as the Canucks scored four goals from 10 advantages in manpower and all the Flame goals came with Vancouver short-handed. Canucks' outstanding rookie Trevor Linden emerged as the Vancouver leader with a goal and three assists as the series returned to Calgary on even terms at two games apiece.

Sergei Priakin, who became the first Soviet player to play an NHL playoff game in Game 4 (his only game played in the 1989 playoffs), Jiri Hrdina, and Lanny McDonald were back out of the lineup for the fifth game in Calgary as Crisp returned to the unit that began the playoffs.

The series fostered bitter feelings as it progressed. Vancouver coach Bob McCammon at one point called the Flames the dirtiest team in the league, and in the counter-accusations the Flames charged the Canucks with foul play. The fifth game fuelled the fire. On the scoreboard, the Flames won the game, 4–0, with Vernon turning aside 18 shots while Calgary fired 40 at Steve Weeks. Mullen returned to the lineup and potted one of the goals. But the Flames paid a very heavy price for the 3–2 series edge as Gary Suter suffered a broken jaw and Dana Murzyn injured a knee. Suter, just returning to form after the appendectomy that resulted in a 15-pound loss, had played his final game of the '89 playoffs. The news on Murzyn provided relief – the knee injury was not serious and he returned for the seventh game.

The Canucks forced the deciding game with their 6–3 home-ice triumph on April 13. This was the game in which Al MacInnis launched what would become a record for defencemen – a 17-game scoring streak. MacInnis's first-period goal provided hopes the Flames might eliminate the Canucks. But Vancouver exploded for four second-period goals, including three in a span of two minutes and 18 seconds, to tie the series. Canucks' defenceman Garth Butcher, who hadn't scored a goal throughout the regular season, notched the game winner. Calgary's list of casualties grew by one when Mark Hunter sustained a broken hand. He wouldn't return until the Stanley Cup Final.

The Canucks headed to Calgary for the seventh game feeling they had the Flames right where they wanted them – a one-shot decide-it-all situation. They were huge underdogs and they knew the pressure to win rested with the Flames.

In the dressing room the morning of the deciding game, the Flames were a sombre group, realizing that the series had gone far beyond what anyone anticipated. Now that it was to this stage, they knew they'd better win or there would be a lot of summer-time questions.

The strain, at times like this, rests most on the goaltenders. Haunted by the unfair criticism for failure a year earlier, Mike Vernon would face the challenge of his hockey life a few hours later ... and emerge the hero.

"I can't say enough about Vernie and the way he came up with those outstanding saves," MacInnis said. "We woke up on the Sunday morning after the game and saw all that snow on the ground in Calgary and we knew it was too early to be playing golf. We were really glad to knock off the Canucks and move on to the next series."

The Canucks were gone but by no means forgotten.

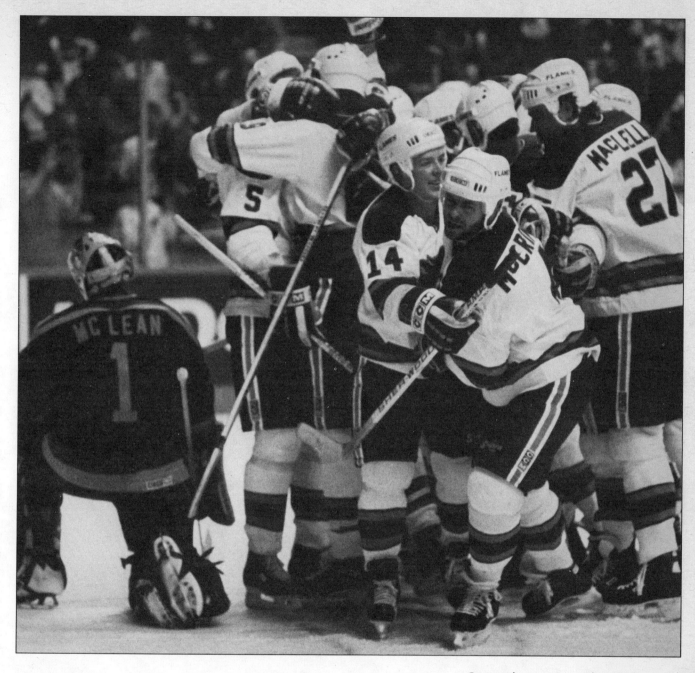

Guess who won? . . . The much-relieved Calgary Flames, fully extended to eliminate the Canucks, wearily congratulate each other after Joel Otto's over-time goal in Game 7. Vancouver goalie Kirk McLean is still too numb to leave his goal crease. *(Calgary Sun photo)*

Getting started . . . Joe
Nieuwendyk's goal had co-captain Jim Peplinski rejoicing as he
jammed the goalmouth in
Calgary's 5–2 verdict over the
Canucks in Game 2 of their
series. (Calgary Sun photo)

The thrill of victory . . . Joel Otto scores one of the biggest goals in Flames' history – perhaps the biggest – as Jim Peplinski's centred pass caromed off his skate and past Vancouver goalie Kirk McLean. Otto's overtime goal shattered the Canucks' hopes for an upset – and kept the Flames' dreams for the Stanley Cup alive. *(Calgary Sun photo)*

Above: Jam up in the crease . . . Mark Hunter plays it ruggedly as proven by this goalmouth pile up against the Vancouver Canucks. (*Calgary Sun photo*)

Inset: Take that . . . Jamie Macoun, who made a remarkable comeback in 1988-89, shows his liking for physical combat in this collision with Vancouver's Trevor Linden during Game 2 of their series. (*Calgary Sun photo*)

Above: Canucks were tough . . . Written off by many, the Vancouver Canucks proved to be almost too much to handle. Here Garth Butcher sends a message out to Theoren Fleury during Game 5, won by Calgary, 4–0. *(Calgary Sun photo)*

Inset: Looking for daylight . . . Mark Hunter tries to turn up a notch and escape Vancouver's Paul Reinhart. *(Calgary Sun photo)*

Whoopee! . . . Theoren Fleury
celebrates in arms of Tim Hunter
after scoring a key goal in the
Flames' second-game win in the
Vancouver series. *(Calgary Sun
photo)*

How Sweep It Is!

he 1988-89 Smythe Division playoffs were not predictable. Sure, the odds-on favourite Calgary Flames emerged from the pack, but the manner in which they advanced through each round bore little resemblance to what one might have expected. They were life and – scared to – death against the Vancouver Canucks and then they quickly eliminated the Los Angeles Kings in four games.

Wayne Gretzky and the Kings swept? Casey Stengel's "Who'da thunk it?" seems to best describe the Flames' roller-coaster ride through the Smythe. The addition of Gretzky in the mammoth trade in the summer of 1988 made the Kings Stanley Cup contenders. They reinforced those beliefs by overcoming a deficit of three games to one and sending Gretzky's old mates, the defending champion Edmonton Oilers, off to an early summer.

While the Flames completed their overtime conquest of the Canucks, the Great Western Forum was sheer bedlam as the Kings were in the process of taking the seventh game over the Oilers with Mr. Gretzky leading the way to a very sweet victory.

The Kings, with Gretzky, went from 68 points and 18th in the overall standings in 1987-88 to 92 points and fourth overall in 1988-89. In the process, they created hockey hysteria in wonderful, sunny California, setting a team attendance record of 595,000 for an average of 14,875, with 24 sellouts. The previous year, the Kings drew 466,677 spectators for an average of 11,667 a game and flashed the SRO sign a mere five times. The Great Western Forum was also hopping during the '88-89 playoffs as the Kings sold out all six post-season games.

Following their series victory over Edmonton, hockey aspirations reached new heights. And the Kings had every reason to be optimistic about their chances against Calgary, especially since Vancouver pushed the Flames to the limit. In this case, though, the regular-season pattern set by the Kings and the Flames prevailed. They'd met eight times with the Flames winning six, including all four at the Saddledome.

No other series the Flames played during the regular season produced as many goals as their encounters with the Kings. Calgary outscored Los Angeles 52–34 – 27–13 at the Saddledome. The Flames had also drubbed the Kings by an 11–4 count at Calgary early in the season and by 9–3 at Los Angeles late in the season. Doug Gilmour and Joey Mullen had scorched the Kings all season. Mullen had totalled 21 points (14 goals) through the eight games against the Kings and equalled a Calgary record for most points in a game (six) in one of the meetings between the two clubs. Gilmour had counted 10 assists in the seven games he played against L.A.

After the Flames' tussle with Vancouver and the Kings' knockout of the Oilers, this series should have been close. The opening game at the Saddledome suggested it would be. The Flames started the Smythe Division final in the same manner they played most of the Canucks' series – tense. Kings' coach Robbie Ftorek, who would be dismissed by Los Angeles eight days after this series, didn't seem very intimidated by the Flames' Sea of Red colour support among the fans in the Saddledome because he wore a red sweater for that opening game. It would prove to be the closest the Kings would come to winning.

They carried a 3–2 lead into the final period thanks to a long-shot goal by Jim Wiemer that Mike Vernon compared to "a Phil Niekro knuckle curveball type thing – it handcuffed me." Calgary sent the game into overtime on a fluke goal of its own with a minute and 36 seconds left in regulation time. The puck, shot into the Kings' zone, went around the end glass and caromed in front of the net to Gary Roberts, who slammed the equalizer past a startled Kelly Hrudey.

The overtime generated some excellent chances at both ends, with Gretzky firing a shot reminiscent of last year's overtime winner – only this missed just over the crossbar. Marty McSorley, covering for the out-of-position Hrudey, took a sure goal away from Mullen. Mullen's line fired the winner a short time later when Colin Patterson stripped the puck from McSorley and relayed it to Gilmour, who took care of business in the 4–3 win.

This game symbolized the start of an unbelievable performance by Gilmour. Ineffective against Vancouver and refusing to use his abscessed jaw as an excuse, Gilmour played as many predicted he would. He not only shadowed Gretzky but outscored him – and the pattern continued into the other rounds. Despite being goal-less against Vancouver and drawing the top guns for checking assignments, Gilmour finished with 11 goals and 11 assists in 22 playoff games. Mullen would finish with 24 points, including a playoff-leading 16 goals, while Patterson turned in 13 points, making the unit Calgary's highest scoring in the playoffs.

"I felt badly in the first series because I just didn't play well," Gilmour said. "I'm glad I had a second chance to help the team."

Unable to produce a winning streak since their last four games of the regular season, the Flames came to life with those back-to-back overtime wins over Vancouver and L.A. Before losing in the second game of the next round, the Flames ran off a six-game winning streak.

The second game against the Kings became an 8–3 Calgary rout with a bit of the unusual. The Flames were in front 4–0 before the game was 12 minutes old as Gilmour showed the way with two goals. During this first period, the Kings' Bernie Nicholls decked Vernon with a blow he termed "as hard as I hit anybody." The play was swinging up ice at this time and unbeknownst to the officials, Jim (Bearcat) Murray – the only trainer in the NHL with cleated runners – had jumped onto the ice and run to aid the fallen Vernon. As Murray tended to Vernon, Gilmour scored another goal for the Flames.

"That certainly was the oddest thing that happened to us throughout the year," Lanny McDonald said.

Naturally, the incident promoted quips about Bearcat wanting more ice time but the bottom line, in his opinion, was performing his duty. "I didn't know a thing about the goal or anything else," he said. "I saw Vernie fall, try to get up and fall again so I went to help him."

If the Flames needed additional inspiration in this game it came from McDonald, who faced the challenge during some brawling when the game got out of hand. McDonald rarely engages in such activity, but he showed that he and his teammates would not be pushed around.

The series then switched to Los Angeles, where Kings' owner Bruce McNall welcomed another star-studded list of celebrities to the Great Western Forum. The stars on ice proved to be the Flames once more. Goals by Jamie Macoun and Joel Otto in the first period carried into the third period, when the Kings narrowed the lead on an early goal by Tom Laidlaw. Then L.A. turned up their attack, firing 11 unanswered shots at Vernon during one stretch, but the Calgary goalie met the challenge, robbing Steve Kasper and Dale Degray of what looked to be sure goals.

The Flames were without Mullen for over 40 minutes after he was charged by Ken Baumgartner in the first period. Once the dizziness subsided and Mullen felt ready, he returned to action with Calgary up 3–2. He promptly engineered Gilmour's second goal of the game, then fired the final tally in the Flames' 5–2 triumph, which gave them a 3–0 series lead. "I got my revenge the best way I know how – with an assist and that goal," Mullen said. "And they were key goals for us because they put the game away."

The Kings attempted to play it tough in this game, especially with the Flames' more diminutive players. When I asked Coach Terry Crisp about the attacks on his smaller players, he said: "It depends on what you mean by smaller players … in stature or in heart? We don't have any small players on our team."

The situation confronting Gretzky was not a familiar one for him. For the second time in his career – and first time since 1983 – Gretzky was with a team that found itself behind 3–0 in a playoff series. "I don't like where we are," Gretzky said. "But the Flames are playing extremely well and deserve a lot of credit."

Held goalless through the first three games of the series, Gretzky finally scored in the fourth game, on April 24. That goal made him the all-time leading scorer in Stanley Cup action, but it wasn't enough as the Flames completed the sweep with a 5–3 win. Steve Duchesne and Gretzky for the Kings, Mullen and Roberts for the Flames, traded first-period goals. Joe Nieuwendyk sent the Flames ahead after two before Mullen and Roberts (empty-netter) sealed the Kings' fate in the third and nullified a second goal by Duchesne. Rob Ramage had a major part in the win, supplying four assists and making a key save on Steve Kasper with Vernon out of position in the second period.

The series produced some criticism of Vernon by Nicholls, but as much as Nicholls tried, the Flames' goalie would not take the bait. "I think Bernie's a little frustrated," Vernon said. "If anybody should say something it should be me, but I won't."

The handshakes on the ice following the game led to an exchange of congratulations between two of the game's outstanding players, Gretzky and McDonald. McDonald provided salutations for Gretzky's record-setting goal while Wayne told Lanny he hoped he'd go all the way to a Stanley Cup win. Lanny would tell me later that Gretzky telephoned his home immediately after the Flames won the Stanley Cup and talked to a couple of his children. Gretzky told them he was very proud and happy that their dad was able to play on a Stanley Cup winner after 16 seasons in the NHL. The very next day, after the Stanley Cup win, Gretzky reached Lanny and personally congratulated him for that splendid accomplishment.

Wayne Gretzky isn't called The Great One for nothing, you know.

Great coverage . . . Doug
Gilmour and Wayne Gretzky,
friends off the ice, play it tough
on the ice. *(Brad Watson photo)*

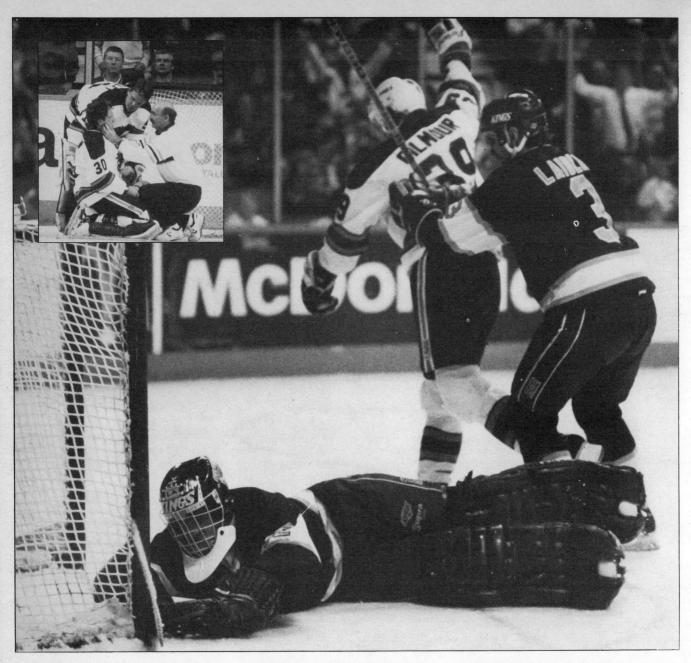

Above: Kings' heartbreaker . . . Doug Gilmour's overtime goal past Kelly Hrudey sank the Kings in the first game of the Smythe Division final. *(Calgary Sun photo)*

Inset: Bearcat to the rescue . . . This incident will go down as one of the oddest of all time. After Mike Vernon was knocked to the ice by the King's Bernie Nicholls, trainer Jim (Bearcat) Murray charged onto the ice as the play moved into the Kings' zone and Doug Gilmour scored. The Flames rolled to an 8–3 win in Game 2 of the Los Angeles series.

Murray, seen tending to Vernon with backup Rick Wamsley after the Gilmour goal, ensured that Vernon finished the game. *(Calgary Sun photo)*

Boy, did we ever need that! . . . Flames' forward Gary Roberts gets up behind the Los Angeles Kings' net after sending the first game of the Smythe Division final into overtime with his goal late in the third period. Doug Gilmour then won it in overtime, 4–3, starting the Flames on their way to a four-game ouster of L.A. *(Calgary Sun photo)*

On guard . . . Flames' defence-
man Ric Nattress fends off a
Kings' player while goalie Mike
Vernon watches the puck.
(Calgary Sun photo)

Kissing the Black-hawks Good-bye

he trip home from Los Angeles permitted time for the Calgary Flames to savour their crowning of the Kings. In some ways, with Wayne Gretzky in the line-up, it was sweet revenge for Calgary's four-game loss to Edmonton in 1988. That debacle had lingered in the Calgarians' minds throughout the off-season and for the entire 1988-89 term. Finally, it was laid to rest.

Mike Vernon felt particularly vindicated by the sweep of the Kings. "I was very, very frustrated in losing to the Oilers and what we had to endure last summer," he told me. "Everywhere I'd go to play golf last summer, all I heard about was the four-straight loss so this is really nice that we can come around and beat a team like Los Angeles in four."

Vernon noted the Flames were peaking at the right time, and yielding only 11 goals against the Kings – the highest scoring team during the NHL's regular season – proved that the defensive, disciplined style installed by the coaching staff returned dividends.

The Flames' next mission was the Clarence Campbell Conference final against the Norris Division-winning Chicago Blackhawks. Chicago had intentions of becoming the first Norris team to win the conference championship since the system began with the realignment in 1981-82. The Blackhawks, 27–41–12 for 66 points, emerged from the NHL's weakest division (frequently referred to as the Snorris Division) after qualifying for the playoffs on the final night of the regular season. They then impressively sidelined the Detroit Red Wings and the St. Louis Blues in the playoffs.

Two factors stressed the fact the Flames couldn't take the Blackhawks lightly. First, under coach Mike Keenan, Chicago became more competitive with a reasonably respectable 17–16–7 second-half record. Also, the Vancouver Canucks, only eight points better than the Blackhawks, almost bumped Calgary from the playoffs in the opening round.

The May 2 opener at the Saddledome, won 3–0 by the home side, was the Flames' sixth consecutive playoff victory, and Vernon picked up his third playoff shutout, one shy of the Stanley Cup record. Alain Chevrier, who played a major role in Chicago's turnaround after he was obtained from Winnipeg, surrendered a long goal to Jamie Macoun in the first period for what proved to be the winner. Calgary outshot Chicago, 39–19, but Chevrier kept the visitors close. And Joe Nieuwendyk had a taste of the misfortune that awaited him during this and the next playoff round when a skate blade cut him for three stitches under the chin and a high stick to the face put him on the bench briefly. Despite these annoyances, Nieuwendyk worked himself free after taking a pass from Al MacInnis and scored the Flames' only goal of the second period. Brian MacLellan sealed the workmanlike victory with the only third-period goal.

The game produced an unusual incident when Tim Hunter picked up a penalty – while sitting on the Flames' bench – as he tapped Steve Thomas on the shoulder with his stick. Unfortunately for Hunter, referee Dave Newell witnessed the incident.

The reviews on the Blackhawks following the opening game loss were not kind. From fans to the media, the Blackhawks were made the fall guys for what was perceived as a poor playoff structure when, the critics said, Chicago had no business being in the NHL's final four. To their credit, the Blackhawks used the putdowns to their advantage, even pinning a *Calgary Sun* headline to the board in their dressing room. That headline read: "Bring on the Canadiens."

Taken for dead, the inspired Blackhawks roared to a 3–0 lead in just over six minutes of Game 2, then held on for a 4–2 decision. Steve Larmer, Denis Savard, Steve Thomas, and Trent Yawney scored for Chicago while Hakan Loob and Joey Mullen responded for the Flames.

Keenan also used a psychological ploy between the first two games by complaining about a lack of dressing-room space at the Saddledome, and his Blackhawks returned home tied with Calgary – and with home-ice advantage now in their favour. And Chicago Stadium's loud fans, coaxed by the sounds of that huge old pipe organ and that ear-shattering horn after each Chicago goal, can be the most intimidating in hockey.

The third game of the series was a chippy affair in which Hakan Loob, Joe Mullen, and Nieuwendyk were injured at various times because of stick work. They returned and contributed to the Flames'

"C" of champions . . . Flames'
fans lined the streets in huge
numbers for the victory parade.
(*Calgary Sun photo*)

Olympic Plaza salute . . . The
Flames' players were honoured
in front of a large audience –
despite damp, chilly weather.
(Calgary Sun photo)

Sign of the times . . . Goalie Mike Vernon proudly waves the sign created by a Flames' fan on the occasion of the victory parade. Along with Vernon are team-mates Gary Suter (20), Gary Roberts (10), and Joe Nieuwendyk (25). *(Calgary Sun photo)*

Here it is . . . Co-captains Tim Hunter, Lanny McDonald, and Jim Peplinski proudly display the Stanley Cup for the fans. *(Calgary Sun photo)*

5–2 win, but the Blackhawks' Wayne Presley suffered a dislocated shoulder when checked into the boards and was lost for the series.

Mullen and Nieuwendyk with goals in a first period dominated by Calgary and Theoren Fleury in the second, between Chicago goals by Steve Konroyd and Troy Murray, sent the game into the third period with the Flames ahead 3–2. Loob's goal just past the midway point of the third period provided insurance and Mullen's empty-netter closed the door on the Blackhawks, who were unable to do any damage in the third period despite a 12–2 edge in shots.

Referee Don Koharski left the game with 51 seconds to go in the first period after injuring his neck when he lost his balance and fell into the boards. His replacement, Bill McCreary, had his hands full in the heated affair, which concluded with a brawl as the horn sounded to end the game. The main principles in the scrap were Jim Peplinski and Dave Manson. The aftermath of this incident resulted in an investigation the next day (Sunday, May 7) by NHL executive vice-president Brian O'Neill, who ruled there was no clear-cut instigator in the fight and, therefore, a suspension to Peplinski was not warranted. This decision infuriated Keenan, who again appeared to play on this to motivate his club.

While all this transpired, the Flames' Colin Patterson chalked up quite a few air miles in a short period of time. Patterson returned to Calgary to be with his wife, Sherry, who'd given birth to their first child, Stephanie, at 3 a.m. on Sunday. Patterson had played the first game in Chicago, caught an early-morning flight home, then returned to Chicago Monday morning for the fourth game that night.

Another intense affair occurred in this next game. Once again, Nieuwendyk's courage in the wake of a painful injury provided inspiration. As he veered toward the Chicago net in the second period, Konroyd's stick caught him flush on the mouth and cut his tongue for seven stitches and loosened his bottom front teeth. Nieuwendyk's absence became even more serious when Joel Otto lost his discipline and was ejected for slashing Manson at 8:46 of the second period. For a time, the Flames operated with two centres (Doug Gilmour and Theoren Fleury), with Peplinski and Gary Roberts taking the occasional turn at centre. When Nieuwendyk returned and performed exceptionally despite the throbbing pain, the Flames received a morale boost.

Savard and Gilmour scored second-period power-play goals that stood up through the third period. A tripping penalty to Roberts at 11:43 of overtime gave the Blackhawks a glorious opportunity to win, but the Flames killed the disadvantage in textbook fashion. The Flames had just returned to full strength when Yawney was nabbed for delay of the game at 13:57 after he'd caught the puck in his glove and threw it into the Calgary zone. With Yawney serving time, Al MacInnis blasted the winner past Chevrier and Calgary's 2–1 decision propelled the team to a 3–1 series lead.

Coach Terry Crisp's elation at the deciding goal was there for all to see – he climbed the glass behind the Calgary bench, leaned over, and kissed Norma MacNeil, the wife of Flames' assistant GM Al MacNeil. The Kissing Bandit, Crisp, had thus provided another memorable twist to the Flames' march of '89 as columnists, in particular, had some fun with the incident. Actually, Crisp had been looking for his wife, Sheila, but she was another five or six rows back. Sheila didn't mind that Terry, in his excitement at winning, kissed Norma. "He came over and kissed me later when he saw me in the corridor," Sheila said.

For his part, MacInnis continued to be the consistent offensive – and defensive – general for the Flames. Of his winning goal, he said: "I just wound up and wanted to get the puck in the direction of the net and hoped something would happen with it – and it sure did."

Firmly in control, the Flames captured their second Campbell Conference Bowl on Wednesday, May 10, with a 3–1 home-ice triumph. The Flames outshot Chicago 43–21 for the game, but the score was tied 1–1 heading into the third period on goals by Nieuwendyk in the first and Mike Hudson in the second.

Brian MacLellan tipped a Ric Nattress shot past the stubborn Chevrier for the game winner and Nieuwendyk's late goal in the third period clinched the trip to the Stanley Cup Final.

Nieuwendyk, wearing a protective mask specially designed by Flames' equipment manager Bobby Stewart, said after the game he hoped the Flames would play Montreal in the Final. The Canadiens, after eliminating Hartford and Boston, were ahead in their series with Philadelphia, 3–2, with a game at the Spectrum the next night. "It would be great if the two best teams in hockey during the regular season get into the Stanley Cup Final and settle that issue," Nieuwendyk said.

And that's exactly what would happen.

Ya, Baby, What a Feeling!

It doesn't take much in broadcasting to be remembered for saying something at the height of an emotional moment. That happened to me on April 30, 1986, when the Calgary Flames won the seventh game of the Smythe Division final against the Edmonton Oilers.

In essence, beating Edmonton was Calgary's Stanley Cup triumph that year. The Flames went on to lose the Stanley Cup Final to Montreal, but they had accomplished the unexpected by dumping their bitter rivals, the Oilers. I couldn't resist saying on the night of their most glorious moment: "The Flames have climbed the mountain ... Ya, baby!"

Well, the "Ya, baby" has stuck with me ever since. The Calgary players and listeners to our broadcasts frequently asked me since that April 30, 1986, night when I'd use it again. I can't go anywhere and be introduced at a function without someone mentioning the man who coined "Ya, baby!" And in this year's playoffs, some Flame players asked me after the Vancouver and Chicago series whether I'd uttered that saying. My response? Wait for the appropriate time ...

The Stanley Cup victory over the Canadiens became that moment. And in the immediate post-game broadcast I referred to them as "The Eternal Flames" because they completed a storybook season that will never be forgotten. On the ice during the celebrations, several Flame players yelled out their own "Ya, baby!" now that they would go down in hockey history as Stanley Cup champions of 1988-89.

"Looking back on it, we were a lot more confident this year than we were in 1986," Lanny McDonald said. "We were just happy to be in the Stanley Cup Final in 1986. This year we were really afraid to lose because people expected us to win and, what's more, we expected ourselves to win.

"I really don't know if we expected ourselves to win in 1986. I mean, we got the big parade and everything in 1986 but we really didn't want it until we won. The difference was it was all or nothing for us in '89."

While the Flames had their legion of supporters, it seemed the prognosticators who follow hockey around the NHL circuit gave the edge in the 1989 Final to Montreal. The Canadiens had, after all, defeated Calgary in 1986 and taken two of three head-to-head clashes with the Flames in 1988-89, both wins coming in the almost invincible Saddledome.

The convictions went beyond that, though, as the attitude prevailed that the Canadiens, or Les Glorieux as they are called in the French-language media, are unbeatable in the Stanley Cup Final. Twenty-three Stanley Cups ... never losing a Stanley Cup Final on home ice ... not relinquishing a Stanley Cup Final since being conquered by Toronto in 1967 ... winning the Cup in 1968, 1969, 1971, 1973, 1976, 1977, 1978, 1979, and, of course, 1986. And then there were the legends of Habs Joliat, Hainsworth, Morenz, Blake, Lach, Rocket Richard, Pocket Rocket Richard, Plante, Harvey, Beliveau, Lafleur, Dryden ... The list is endless, really.

"We're playing the 1989 Canadiens," said Flames' assistant coach Doug Risebrough, a Hab from 1974 to 1982. "Morenz, Beliveau, and the Rocket were with other Canadien teams. And, furthermore, I know from personal experience there are no ghosts in the Montreal Forum. The Canadien teams I played on that won the Stanley Cup did it with talent and hard, hard work." Risebrough conveyed this very message to the Flame players prior to the start of the Final, sensing perhaps that the Flames of '86 had been awestruck by the Canadien tradition.

The 1989 Stanley Cup Final began on Mother's Day, Sunday, May 14. As the top two teams in the NHL regular season – and the two best defensive teams in the league (Montreal yielded 218 goals; Calgary had 226 goals against) – went at each other they shocked everyone by striking for four goals within 10:02 of referee Andy van Hellemond dropping the puck to start the game.

Stephane Richer shot the Canadiens ahead just before the three-minute mark on a power play but goals by Al MacInnis on the power play at 6:51 and on a three-on-one break at 8:43 had Calgary fans buzzing. Joel Otto figured in on both MacInnis goals, showing once more how he thrives in pressure situations. MacInnis, in picking up at least a point in his 12th consecutive playoff game, also displayed his true grit by his response to what could just as well have been a blow to his confidence. Richer stepped around the Flames' defenceman for that first goal, but rather than let it bother him, MacInnis took charge and more than made up for the Montreal score.

Larry Robinson supplied the equalizer before the teams finally settled into the well-played, disciplined style that persisted in their regular-season and playoff successes. Theoren Fleury settled the issue when he propelled a shot through the legs of Patrick Roy, the five-hole as it is known in hockey, midway through the second period. For the game, Calgary outshot the Canadiens, 35–31, as Mike Vernon and Roy played brilliantly in an exciting start for the 1989 Final.

Fleury was, to say the least, thrilled to supply the winning goal in his first Stanley Cup Final game. But there was more to it for him than that, for he had grown up in Russell, Manitoba, as a staunch Canadiens' supporter, idolizing Guy Lafleur and Jacques Lemaire. A friend of his father's had given Theoren a Canadiens' sweater, which he wore all the time on outdoor rinks and in his minor hockey endeavours. Now, there he was, sinking his favourite team in the first game of the Final. Wouldn't it be something if he could accomplish that again in the deciding game?

"Well, I hope it's Lanny McDonald who scores the winning goal in the clinching game," Fleury said, not realizing he wasn't far off the mark with that thought.

The Saddledome crowd was the noisiest I had ever heard it during the final game of the Chicago series and in the first game against Montreal. Caught up in the enthusiasm and ahead 1–0 in the series, MacInnis remarked to me: "I can feel it … I think we're going to have great things here."

The Canadiens, meanwhile, became embroiled in an internal controversy when winger Claude Lemieux toppled in melodramatic agony after a mild hit by Jamie Macoun. No one fell for the dive except Lemieux, who was not pleased when none of his teammates or the Montreal training staff came to his aid. Lemieux admitted later the dive was indeed just that, and though officials responded positively to his acting during his very impressive 1986 playoff campaign, they ignored it this year.

When it was learned between games that Lemieux would be scratched for the second game, a French-language daily accused Montreal Coach Pat Burns of not playing Lemieux because the coach was anti-Francophone. Burns, fully bilingual, refuted any such thing, stating that his mother was French Canadian.

Instead of wilting over this confrontation, the Canadiens responded with a 4–2 victory on Wednesday, May 18. It should be noted that, as things evolved, the Canadiens won their two games in the series with Lemieux not dressed and lost all four in which he did play.

The Canadiens, outshot 24–15 after two periods and 16–4 in the second period alone, were kept in the game by Roy and capitalized on the few opportunities they had. "We didn't give Montreal a lot of chances but Montreal doesn't need a lot of chances," coach Terry Crisp said after the game. "They had 12, maybe 14, chances and scored four goals. That's the sign of a good team."

Robinson, in the first period, and Bobby Smith, early in the second on a power play, shot the Canadiens ahead by two before Joe Nieuwendyk and Otto, on the power play, tied the score before the end of the second. Goals by Canadiens' leader Chris Chelios and Russ Courtnall a minute and 34 seconds apart midway through the third period sealed the game for Montreal. Vernon criticized himself on the Chelios winner, saying: "There's no question about it. I blew it. I should have stopped that puck but I just didn't get there."

As the series headed to Montreal for the third and fourth games, the media attention focused on the startling similarity in pattern this series was taking to that of the 1986 showdown. Like 1986, the first two games were played in Calgary, and the Flames won the opening game but lost the second. If history repeated itself, the Canadiens would win Games 3 and 4 at the Forum, then wrap up the series in Game 5 at Calgary.

Flames' president/general manager Cliff Fletcher had reason to think differently. "No, I'm not worried with the split because we played very well in the two games at home and easily could have won them both," he said. "We're a far more mature team than we were in 1986. We knew from the beginning that this was going to be a long series and we're not worried about playing in the Montreal Forum."

Amid their march to the Stanley Cup Final the Flames, like most teams, developed quite a few superstitions. Included among them was that most of the players now sported beards; another became wearing yellow bracelets, an idea Nieuwendyk borrowed from the New York Mets of 1988. Doug Gilmour claimed Joey was too cheap to go out and buy them so he took it upon himself to outfit the team with bracelets for a reported $2 each. Crisp later supplemented the team bracelet with one from his daughter, Caley.

Gilmour and fellow Kingston, Ontario, product Don Cherry developed another superstition that actually goes back four seasons. It seems that each time Gilmour and Cherry shook hands before a game, Gilmour would respond with a big game that, more often than not, has included at least two goals. It's difficult to surmise who had more fun with this one, Gilmour or Cherry.

"I'll tell you, it was something else ... scary, really," Cherry said. "It started about four years ago when he was in St. Louis and they were playing Minnesota in the playoffs. There was a national telecast going back to Kingston and I told Dougie I'd love to say something about him for his folks but he wasn't doing anything. So I shook hands and wished him good luck." That night, Gilmour recorded five assists – and couldn't wait to get on television for the post-game interview.

"One time this year in the Chicago series," Cherry said, "I shook hands with him after the first period, then went on television and said because we didn't shake hands before the game, he'd get one goal – and that's what he did.

"The funniest thing is that when the series got to Montreal, he was waiting for me all the time. He wouldn't go on the ice until we shook hands. And if he couldn't find me, he'd send someone to find me. That last game, he had one goal going into the final minutes and I thought for sure he'd only finish with the one. But then he scored into the empty net!"

There was nothing superstitious about the proficiency of Gilmour. In the eyes of Cherry and other noted hockey experts, the Flames' centre earned high praise. "Serge Savard (Montreal GM) said that he thought Gilmour was the difference in the Final series," Cherry noted. "Guys like Harry Neale, Scotty Bowman, and I couldn't believe how this guy never seemed to tire. Hit him, and he'd bounce back up like nothing happened. Bowman said Gilmour reminded him of Davey Keon ... tireless skaters who gave their all and never got weary."

Goalie Rick Wamsley is credited with a superstition assist as he outwaited Courtnall during the pre-game warmup in the sixth game of the series in Montreal. Courtnall wanted to do his customary shooting of the puck into the empty enemy net but Wamsley prevented it by refusing to leave. The Canadiens' forward was finally told to leave the ice by an arena attendant.

The pursuit of championships is full of stories such as these, but the bottom line always comes down to consistently sound hockey over a long period of time. These teams certainly carried on with that display in the third-game marathon, decided by Ryan Walter's goal at 18:08 of the second overtime, which came just as a controversial penalty to Mark Hunter ended, providing a 4–3 Montreal victory and 2–1 series lead for the Habs. It was the longest game in Flames' history and perhaps the most exciting overtime game I had ever seen.

Referee Kerry Fraser assessed a minor to Hunter, playing his first game since breaking a hand in the sixth game against Vancouver, for boarding Shayne Corson. While the Canadiens' goal did not officially come on the power play, it developed with Hunter in the penalty box for a foul he – and the Flames – insisted should not have been called.

The game was played in two clearly defined segments – regulation time, which definitely belonged to the Flames, and overtime, which was decidedly owned by the Canadiens. In familiar pattern, despite these variances, the clubs were close on the scoreboard all night, thanks to goaltenders Vernon and Roy.

Mike McPhee and Joey Mullen, who snapped a four-game goalless streak that matched his longest of the season, exchanged first-period goals and then Mullen put the Flames ahead after two. Smith squared the count once more early in the third but the Flames appeared to have things in control when Gilmour made it 3–2 with under seven minutes to go in regulation time.

A couple of last-minute miscues let the Canadiens off the hook; first Mullen missed an empty net with Roy on the bench for a sixth attacker and then a failed clearing attempt by Brad McCrimmon resulted in Mats Naslund slapping a knuckleball shot past Vernon. The Canadiens were outshot 28–17 in regulation time but stormed out early in overtime and were deprived of scoring early by Vernon. By the time Walter ended the drama, Montreal had an 18–9 edge in shots during the overtime.

To be sure, the Flames were upset over the penalty call to Hunter, but the lesson learned by Crisp in a regular-season loss to Montreal for which he blamed himself resulted in a composed post-game reaction to the incident. Rather than making the whole affair a crutch to lean on, the Flames used it as a rallying cry, and this became a vital ingredient in the series turnaround.

The fourth game of the series on Sunday, May 21, loomed as the most pivotal of the entire series. Following the exact form of 1986, the Flames trailed 2–1. Falling behind 3–1 would just about seal their fate.

The day prior to this game, Fletcher, as he very rarely does, addressed the players and asked them to go out and play "a franchise game." He knew the unlimited potential of the club he'd assembled and believed the Calgary operation would receive its biggest boost ever if each player played the game of his life and returned home even in the series. After Game 4 of the Vancouver series Fletcher also spoke to the players, on that occasion on the team bus immediately after the game, stating his belief that they were on the verge of greatness and should not let the opportunity escape.

They won the next game versus Vancouver and they came back to capture that fourth game in Montreal with a tremendous display of character. From then on, the Flames would not be denied, and for the only time all season the Canadiens would lose three consecutive games.

Still, it wasn't easy – none of the Montreal-Calgary battles ever is. The Flames outshot Montreal 13–3 in the first period but couldn't score. Gilmour and Mullen, on the power play, finally penetrated Roy in the second period. The Flames, as in the previous game, appeared in firm control, but Courtnall brought the Canadiens and the fans back to life at the 11-minute mark of the third.

The thinking grew that MacInnis bothered Roy throughout the series with his booming shot, for the Canadiens' goalie often reared back when the Flames' defenceman wound up. That thinking was reinforced when MacInnis blasted a drive past Roy with under two minutes to go.

The lead was safe, right? Wrong.

Mullen banked a shot off the goalpost with Roy on the bench for an extra attacker and the Canadiens moved up ice to score at 19:33, courtesy of Lemieux. But Mullen would not miss his next empty-net opportunity, scoring the clincher in the 4–2 victory at 19:49. It was a power-play goal because of a silly penalty Lemieux took after his goal, thus taking the momentum away from the Canadiens. The needling Mullen received after the vacant-net capers was totally anticipated as Calgary players noted that Joey is used to scoring with goalies in the net – and would have to practise scoring with them out of the net.

The relieved Flames returned home buoyant … they had shattered the trend of the '86 Final and now could concentrate on mapping out a totally different course.

The Flames were greeted by an excited overflow crowd at the Saddledome for the fifth game on Tuesday, May 23. Overall, this probably was the worst game the Flames played in the Final, but they held off a furious Montreal attack to win 3–2 and take the series lead.

Calgary generated all its offence in the first period, with Otto scoring in the first minute followed by tallies from Mullen and MacInnis, another blast from the blueline that restored the Flames' two-goal cushion. Smith, in the first, and Mike Keane, in the second, brought the Canadiens within one each time but, with Vernon playing splendidly, the Flames protected the key win.

Following the game, one almost had the feeling the Calgary fans knew their team now had the Stanley Cup. Many of them lingered in the lobby area for a long time and we heard cheers continuously throughout our post-game show. The fans outside were also in a celebrative mood. They believed this had been the Flames' final home game of the season, and they were right.

The media, however, offered opposing views to that. I noted when I walked into the media lounge back at the Forum on the night of May 25 the near unanimity that existed regarding a Montreal victory that night. The Flames still had to prove they merited the trust from the media that they could, indeed, capture "the big game." On the other hand, the Canadiens' tradition, so entrenched in the psyche of anyone who followed hockey, loomed rock solid and worthy of backing. On this night, though, history would be altered.

The Flame lineup went through a fine-tuning beginning in Game 3 of the Final when Mark Hunter replaced McDonald. Jiri Hrdina entered the fray in Game 4, subbing for Jim Peplinski. Tim Hunter gave way to Peplinski for Game 5 and then for the deciding game, only 20 minutes before game time, the Flames confirmed that McDonald would play, with Peplinski sitting out. Each player, under personal strain when informed of inactivity on any of these given nights, never pulled the organization apart. And when each received the call, the Flames knew they would receive nothing but the utmost contribution. They earned special praise for the professional manner in which the situation was handled, especially under difficult decision-making circumstances for the coaches.

The Flames, to say the least, were tense for the sixth game ... it was a totally new experience for them, and all the associated championship preparations tested their superstitious minds. The night before the game, Fletcher called MacInnis, Vernon, Otto, and Mullen together and reluctantly explained that if one of them was named winner of the Conn Smythe Trophy as MVP of the playoffs, he stood to earn $10,000 on top of his playoff share of $25,000 and the $3,000 for being named MVP by saying on the ice, after the announcement: "I'm going to Disney World."

This was a promotional deal arranged through the NHL by Disney World. The theme/amusement park has also done similar promotions involving the Super Bowl and World Series MVPs. MacInnis, who would earn the Smythe selection, went through three takes: the first without the Stanley Cup, the other two with it.

On the afternoon of the sixth game, Al Coates met with league officials and the three television networks covering the Final (*Hockey Night in Canada, Soirée du Hockey,* and SportsChannel of America) to review post-game dressing-room procedures in the event the Flames won that night. And the NHL, through its licensing agency, Licensing Corporation of America, had designed a special logo to commemorate the 1989 Stanley Cup playoffs and oversaw the championship graphics that appeared on the caps and T-shirts waiting for the Flames.

Fletcher and Coates both felt awkward knowing of these preparations, fearful of jinxing the situation. Rick Skaggs, the Flames' director of public relations, felt just as queasy over revealing plans outlined by the city of Calgary regarding the Flames' victory parade set for two days later.

The jitters were unwarranted, once the Flames moved into gear after a sluggish start. Tentative and tense prior to the game, the Flames started the game that way but, with Vernon guarding the door, they escaped any early damage, emerging with a 1–0 first-period lead on a goal by Colin Patterson.

The Canadiens offset that in the second period on a fluke goal as a shot by Lemieux went off Vernon's blocker and, when lost by the Calgary goalie, skipped into the net. Given the fact the Flames appeared on the ropes and had just yielded a soft goal, the scene appeared set when McDonald took a holding penalty early in that second period. Once more, Calgary's effective penalty killing neutralized the Montreal power play and, 11 seconds after stepping out of the penalty box, McDonald took a pass from Nieuwendyk and fired a shot to the top shelf for the go-ahead goal. It was vintage McDonald: a tremendous way to score his final goal.

The Canadiens, pulling out all the stops, tried to agitate Vernon by running at him and creating havoc in front of him on numerous occasions. One such reaction proved costly, however, as Courtnall was nabbed for boarding Vernon behind the net at 10:46 of the third period. The Flames knew they were in business for this one when Vernon, wisely, did not retaliate – and neither did any of his mates.

Sixteen seconds later, Gilmour tapped in his own rebound through the gaping five-hole and Calgary appeared ready to uncork that long-awaited champagne. Typically, this game would go down to the final minute because Rick Green, who last scored a playoff goal against Calgary in 1986, sliced the Flames' lead 51 seconds after the Gilmour goal.

MacInnis, his point-scoring streak stretched to 17 games and the first defenceman to win the playoff scoring title, with 31 points, was in the penalty box with Lemieux when Gilmour's empty-net goal at 18:57 put the championship seal on the 4–2 triumph.

The pressure was now off. Cliff Fletcher, who'd watched the third period in the TV room with Flames' video man Gary Taylor and the players who did not play, could now breathe easier. Capitals' general manager David Poile, whom he helped groom in Atlanta and Calgary before subsequently recommending him to Washington, and the Islanders' Bill Torrey, were among the first to congratulate Fletcher.

All those years of waiting for next year had indeed finally arrived – for Fletcher … for McDonald … for the city of Calgary … and for The Eternal Flames.

Welcome Home, Champs!

The special guest on the Calgary Flames' charter flight home had its own special seat.

Mind you, it took some time before Al Murray, the Flames' assistant trainer, snapped the locks on the protective case carrying it. But once that famous mug, the Stanley Cup, was unveiled, each and every Flame, along with wives or girlfriends, got to admire the very symbol of hockey excellence all the way home. Once a distant desire, the Stanley Cup now belongs to the Flames and is theirs to defend.

Electric Avenue still showed the remains of an overnight party that attracted some 25,000 people when the Flames arrived home at 5 a.m. on Friday, May 26. The Flames had turned on the city of Calgary and nothing displayed this more than the front-page headlines that greeted them. The *Calgary Herald* shouted: "FLAMES WIN – Stanley Cup: Ours at last." The *Calgary Sun* proclaimed: "WE DID IT! NO. 1."

Calgary rolled out the red carpet for its "C" of red two days after the championship and, despite freezing rain and unseasonably cold weather, some 50,000 lined the parade route while another 20,000 crammed into Olympic Plaza for the civic reception. "Today," proclaimed Mayor Don Hartman, "is like 10 gold medals rolled into one." Calgary pride had reached its zenith.

The impact of the Flames' Stanley Cup was driven home for me during my off-season travels. On a trip to Florida in July, I was listening to the CBS radio baseball game of the week between the Minnesota Twins and the California Angels. The commentators, Brent Musburger and Johnny Bench, started talking about player numbers, referring to the fact another famous Number 5 (Bench) this year was joining previous others, such as Joe DiMaggio and Brooks Robinson, in the Baseball Hall of Fame.

When Musburger pointed out the significance of Number 9 in hockey, Bench responded: "Well, last year in hockey the big numbers were 99 (Wayne Gretzky) and 66 (Mario Lemieux), but the Calgary Flames were the class team in hockey."

Then, in August, a month prior to the Flames' journey to Czechoslovakia and the Soviet Union for training camp, the *Globe and Mail* reported that *Sovietsky Sport* concluded the Flames were the best hockey team in the world last season.

Excellence is recognized world over and nothing can compare to being *the* champion. The Calgary Flames now know – and appreciate – that.

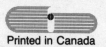

Printed in Canada